D1518283

COLONIAL SETTLEMENTS IN AMERICA

Jamestown
New Amsterdam
Philadelphia
Plymouth
St. Augustine
Santa Fe
Williamsburg
Yerba Buena

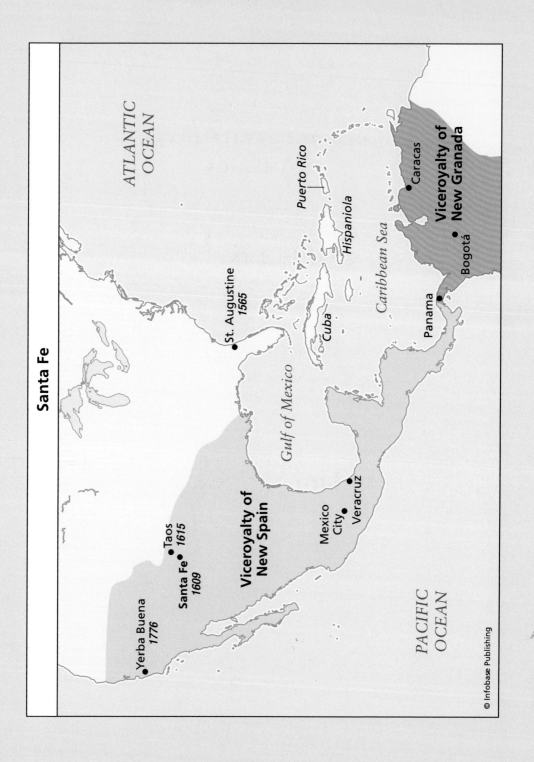

ATLANTIC
OCEAN

Puerto Rico

Hispaniola

Caribbean Sea

Caracas

Viceroyalty of
New Granada

Bogotá

Cuba

Panama

St. Augustine
1565

Gulf of Mexico

Mexico
City
Veracruz

Viceroyalty of
New Spain

Taos
1615

Santa Fe
1609

Yerba Buena
1776

PACIFIC
OCEAN

© Infobase Publishing

COLONIAL SETTLEMENTS
IN AMERICA

Santa Fe

Tim McNeese

CHELSEA HOUSE
PUBLISHERS
An imprint of Infobase Publishing

Frontis: Although Santa Fe was first settled in 1609, it did not become the official capital of Nuevo México until the following year. The Viceroyalty of New Spain is illustrated on this map.

Santa Fe

Chelsea House
An imprint of Infobase Publishing
132 West 31st Street
New York, NY 10001

ISBN-10: 0-7910-9332-8   ISBN-13: 978-0-7910-9332-0

Library of Congress Cataloging-in-Publication Data
McNeese, Tim.
  Santa Fe / Tim McNeese.
    p. cm. — (Colonial settlements in America)
  Includes bibliographical references and index.
  Audience: Grades 7-8.
  ISBN 0-7910-9332-8 (hardcover)
   1. Santa Fe (N.M.)—History—Juvenile literature. 2. New Mexico—History—To 1848—Juvenile literature. 3. Spaniards—New Mexico—History—Juvenile literature. 4. Southwest, New—Discovery and exploration—Spanish—Juvenile literature. I. Title. II. Series.
  F804.S257M38 2007
  978.9'56—dc22   2006028361

Chelsea House books are available at special discounts when purchased in bulk quantities for businesses, associations, institutions, or sales promotions. Please call our Special Sales Department in New York at (212) 967-8800 or (800) 322-8755.

You can find Chelsea House on the World Wide Web at
http://www.chelseahouse.com

Series design by Erika K. Arroyo
Cover design by Ben Peterson

Printed in the United States of America

Bang EJB 10 9 8 7 6 5 4 3 2 1

This book is printed on acid-free paper.

All links and Web addresses were checked and verified to be correct at the time of publication. Because of the dynamic nature of the Web, some addresses and links may have changed since publication and may no longer be valid.

Contents

1

Lost in the Southwest

Shipwrecked! Lost!

The words could only raise fear in the hearts of each half-drowned man who stood on a spring day in the year 1528 on the beaches of modern-day Texas. The men had been part of a small fleet of Spanish ships that had left the Caribbean island of Cuba, en route to the Gulf Coast. Their leader, Pánfilo de Narváez, had been sent by royal officials to establish a colony on the Texas coast, at the mouth of a river known today as the Rio Grande. A sudden storm had blown the ships far off course. One of them had crashed onto rocks, breaking apart and sending it to the ocean floor. The other four ships were badly damaged. Unable to continue the voyage with hundreds of colonists onboard, Narváez had made a fateful decision. He ordered 300 Spaniards ashore, telling them to march along the Gulf Coast to the river they knew then as the *Rio de las Palmas*, the River of Palms.

Hardship would continue to plague the luckless Spaniards during their journey. Those who trudged along the Gulf Coast

Spanish explorer Álvar Núñez Cabeza de Vaca spent eight years wandering what is today Texas and the American Southwest after he was shipwrecked on his way back to Mexico. Finally, in 1536, Cabeza de Vaca encountered a group of Spaniards near the Rio Grande and was taken back to Mexico City, where he and his party were treated like heroes.

were attacked by Native Americans. Many died of disease and hunger. Some deserted and wandered off, never to be seen again. Of the 300 who started their fateful march, only a handful would survive. Among them was a Spanish nobleman named Álvar Núñez Cabeza de Vaca. The story of the survival of the last remnant of the Narváez expedition would stretch along for eight years. Cabeza de Vaca would be the man to tell that story after his return to Mexico in 1536.

BORN OF NOBILITY

Cabeza de Vaca was descended from Spanish nobility. He was a *hidalgo*, a landed aristocrat, who had grown up in a wealthy and privileged world. But once he was cast ashore along the Texas coast in 1528, his aristocratic background could not help him much. He and his comrades had been pitched into a hostile world, filled with unfriendly natives. The lost Spaniards did not know where they were and, as they moved through the frontier wilderness of what is now Texas and New Mexico, they had no idea where they were going or if they would survive. They had, in fact, landed along the coast of East Texas in the vicinity of the Trinity River.

The survivors of the Narváez expedition endured a difficult winter, and they were taken captive by the local Native Americans who held them prisoner for several years. These Spanish survivors were forced to work for their captors, a reversal of the role they were accustomed to holding. Cabeza de Vaca became one member of the party that the Native Americans appeared to get along with. He had limited medical skills and once was able to remove an arrowhead that was embedded in a wounded Indian. But the harsh world the luckless Spaniards had stumbled into continued to take its toll on them. One by one, the Spaniards, overworked, underfed, nearly naked, and burned by the sun, died. In time, Cabeza de Vaca and some of the colonists decided they had better take leave of their captors and find their way back to New Spain.

Cabeza de Vaca was soon on his own, moving into the unknown lands of the American Southwest. In time, he happened upon four other survivors of the Narváez expedition, including three fellow Spaniards and a black Moor who was a convert to Christianity. These four men were living near a different Indian village. When Cabeza de Vaca found them, they were working alongside the Native Americans harvesting pecans along a small river. The locals called the desert stream "the river of nuts." It is believed to have been the Guadalupe River. He and the others set out on foot across the barren Texas landscape. But they were no closer to rescue or finding their way back to Spanish civilization.

YEARS OF ENDLESS WANDERING

Their wanderings continued for several more years. Because the men did not usually know where they were, it is difficult today to track their route across the Southwest. It is thought that they walked across the south-central region of Texas, a route that brought them face-to-face with an animal they had never seen before—the American bison. Later, Cabeza de Vaca would describe the bison in his journal:

> Here also [we] came upon the cows. . . .They appear to me of the size of those in Spain. Their horns are small, like those of Moorish cattle; their hair is very long, like fine wool. . . .Of the small hides, the Indians make blankets to cover themselves with, and of the taller ones they make shoes and targets.[1]

They also passed through the southern parts of modern-day New Mexico and Arizona. They moved through the deserts, the sun baking their naked bodies by day. They became so dark and severely sunburned that "said one castaway, they shed their skins twice a year, like snakes."[2]

Seven years had passed since the capsizing of Narváez's ships. In November 1535, Cabeza de Vaca and his four fellow survivors reached another group of Indian villages, those situated along the banks of the Rio de las Palmas, near modern-day El Paso, Texas. They did not know, of course, that the river they had reached was, in fact, the river on which they were supposed to build their colony.

When they made contact with a new group of Native Americans, Cabeza de Vaca and his men often traded with them. The Spaniards regularly bartered seashells they had picked up along the Gulf Coast for food from these inland natives. Despite their appearance, the lost Europeans also tried to make the Native Americans think they could practice magic. The desert natives often "regarded [the Spaniards] as children of the sun [who] were believed to possess supernatural powers."[3] The Spaniards mimicked the practices of Native American medicine men they had met before and chanted over their Indian "patients," dancing like natives and mouthing the words to Catholic prayers they all knew by heart. Sometimes those they treated did get well. The Native Americans gave them gourd rattles, a symbol used by desert Indian healers.

The bedraggled Spaniards continued on their journey. While they did know that New Spain was to the south, they did not always follow a southerly route. This made their journey longer and kept them from reaching the safety of Spanish settlements. Three impediments kept them moving farther west, rather than south. One reason was because "of natural obstacles they were often deflected northward from their course."[4] The other reasons were equally simple. At least two of Cabeza de Vaca's traveling companions could not swim. When the group reached a river, they sometimes had to move along it until they reached a shallow place where they could all walk across. Also, the men walked from one Indian village to another, searching for food and support. Most of the Native Americans they encountered treated them well. In their miserable condition—hungry and nearly without clothes—the men did not pose a threat to the Native Americans they met in the southwestern deserts.

One tribe that treated them well was the Pima who lived in northwestern Mexico and southern Arizona. They befriended the lost Spaniards and gave them gifts. Among these gifts were five large green ceremonial arrowheads. Cabeza de Vaca thought they were cut from emeralds, but they were probably made from malachite, a common substance in the Southwest. When the Spaniards left the Pima village and headed south on their journey, they were escorted by 600 Pimas.

AT LONG LAST, A RESCUE!

Six months after reaching the Rio Grande—then called the Rio de las Palmas—Cabeza de Vaca and his Spanish comrades were met by a small group of Spaniards riding on horseback. Their meeting was a joyful one. At last, after eight years, the shipwrecked colonists of the Narváez expedition were saved. The horsemen took their companions to the nearest Spanish outpost. The Pimas were still with Cabeza de Vaca and his comrades, but they soon parted company with them. (It appears the Spanish horsemen were in the region looking for natives to enslave. Cabeza de Vaca made certain that the Pimas were allowed to leave and were not enslaved.)

Then the men were taken south to the capital of New Spain, Mexico City. There, they were wined and dined and treated like heroes. They were given an audience with the viceroy, Antonio de Mendoza, who had arrived in the New World only a year earlier. He wanted to hear the details of the amazing journey the small group of Spaniards had experienced in the unknown lands of the Southwest. Cabeza de Vaca was only too willing to recount his tales. But he did not report anything that had not happened. He did not want to embellish his stories just to make the viceroy happy. He spoke well of the lands he had seen: "It is, no doubt, the best land in all these Indias. Indeed, the land needs no circumstance to make it blessed."[5] These words encouraged the viceroy. Mendoza had heard other stories about the lands to the north. He had heard of a tale of Cíbola, the Seven Cities of Gold. Cabeza de Vaca had seen no such cities. However, he had been told by Indians, those living in the Sonoran Desert, of another group of Southwest residents who lived in a city of great wealth. Indian storytellers had related tales of these mysterious people to the north "who lived in large houses and possessed marvelous wares—turquoises, emeralds, even cotton blankets."[6] To the Spanish officials, these lands were filled with great

Ñ.1. El año de 1934. llegò el Excmõ. Senor Don Antonio de Mendoza, Conde, ò Tendilla y fue el primero que tubo el Titulo de Viſò-Rey, y Capitan General á ſtà N.E. goverñò haſta el año de 1949. que paſò de Virrey al Piru.

Antonio de Mendoza (depicted here) was the first viceroy of the Spanish colony of New Spain, a position he held from 1535 to 1550. In 1539, Mendoza sent Francisco Vásquez de Coronado north to explore what is today the American Southwest and search for the Seven Cities of Cíbola, legendary settlements thought to contain vast amounts of treasure.

mysteries, places of legend and huge caches of gold. The region would become modern-day New Mexico and its capital would be known as Santa Fe.

Cabeza de Vaca's words were all that Viceroy Mendoza needed to hear. As far as the Spanish official was concerned, Cabeza de Vaca's tale of a Native American claim to a wealthy city in the distant deserts, beyond forbidding mountains, was persuasive. The Native Americans must have been talking about Cíbola—the Seven Cities of Gold. Perhaps this would be another New World empire of great wealth, such as the Incas of South America or Aztecs of Mexico. The viceroy decided to mount an expedition into the region. And he had just the man for the task—a young hidalgo whom Mendoza had first met in the courts of Spain, a handsome aristocrat, "blue-eyed, with dark blond hair, mustache, and beard, and elegant in figure."[7] Mendoza had brought him to America to serve as his aide. This young man, only 27 years old, had proven himself to be an able soldier, or *conquistador*, having successfully put down an Indian revolt in a village outside Mexico City. He was quite wealthy, having married the daughter of the royal treasurer. He had a reputation for obedience, personal drive, commitment, and honesty. Mendoza would send him to the north in search of Cíbola. His name was Francisco Vásquez de Coronado.

2

Guns and Steel, Horses and Germs

In the fall of 1492, one of the most important events in the history of the previous thousand years took place. Three small ships, sailing in the name of the king of Spain, Ferdinand, were plying ocean waters where no European had ever sailed before—the Caribbean. The date was October 12, 1492. In the early morning hours, a lookout on one of the vessels shouted out that he had spotted land. Those who heard him cried out for joy. A ship's cannon was fired, the prearranged signal to the crews of the sister ships that land had been sighted.

BOUND FOR THE ORIENT

It had been more than four weeks since they had landed at the Canary Islands in the eastern Atlantic Ocean. Since leaving the Canaries, they had sailed across an unknown sea in hopes of reaching the continent of Asia. Their captain, an exceptionally skillful seaman, had told them to expect to be dazzled with the riches of the lands he was taking them to. There was Cipangu (modern-day Japan) with its riches and golden

On August 3, 1492, Genoan explorer Christopher Columbus left
Seville, Spain, and sailed west in search of a route to Asia. Columbus
is depicted here bidding farewell to Queen Isabella shortly before his
departure for the New World.

temples. There was Cathay (modern-day China), a land filled
with exotic spices, jewels, and valuable teakwoods, all treasures that were highly valued in Europe. To the last man, those
onboard the three little ships had dreamed with each passing day of the wealth they would discover when their captain
finally delivered them to the lands of the Orient. And, now,
they were in sight of these lands; or so the men on the three
Spanish-sponsored ships thought.

Their captain, Cristoforo Colombo, as he was called in his
native Genoa, had finally achieved his longtime dream—to
sail west from Europe across the dark waters of the Atlantic

Ocean toward Asia. During the following days, he and his fellow crewmen reached the lands they had spotted that fateful, foggy night. But these lands were not what the Genoan Colombo (in English, his name was Christopher Columbus) and his men expected. As they landed on island after island, they found only poor natives—no riches, no jewels, no gold. What these hearty European mariners could not have known then and would only come to know in time was that they had not reached Asia after all. That continent still lay thousands of miles to the west. Their Genoan leader had completely miscalculated the distance from Spain to Cipangu and Cathay, as well as every other part of Asia. The lands that lay before these newly arrived foreigners were not part of the Asian continent. They were a part of a continent completely unknown to Columbus and his men. They were part of the Western Hemisphere—the Americas.

What Columbus could not have known at the time (he would die more than a decade later still believing he had reached the Orient) was that two oceans—the Atlantic and Pacific—separated Europe from Asia, with two continents separating those oceans from one another. During the 1490s, Columbus made two additional voyages to the Caribbean. During those years, others came, Spaniards mostly, who realized that the world Columbus had reached was not Asia, but one that held riches beyond even the imagination of the most gold-hungry of Europeans. The Spanish would turn Columbus's mistake into a vast New World empire.

THE SPANISH COLONIZE

Following this European "discovery" of the Western Hemisphere, which includes the lands of North, Central, and South America, as well as the islands of the Caribbean, the Spanish government took a singular interest in colonizing as much of this vast, uncharted territory as it could. Despite the natives who lived there, the Spanish believed that every place was for the taking. From the beginning of the 1500s to its end and beyond, Spain would become the new ruler of the western Atlantic. The New World would become the home of the Spanish soldiers called conquistadors; of political leaders and governors who ruled in the name of their monarch; and of holy men, Spanish priests who wanted to spread the name of Jesus and the faith of Christianity. These new people of the New World would be driven by causes as varied as God, gold, and glory. But rule they would, and the indigenous inhabitants of the Western Hemisphere would be forced to submit to them.

Spanish colonization in the Americas would range from the kind to the chaotic; the beautiful to the brutal. Catholic priests might treat one group of American Indians with their good deeds, while another priest might order a village burned, because its people did not accept Christianity as their new religion. One Spanish conquistador might let loose a pack of dogs to tear up any native who challenged his authority, while another might take an Indian woman as his wife. There were those colonists who treated the natives well and with compassion. One such advocate for the native peoples was a Spanish missionary, a Dominican friar named Bartolomé de Las Casas (1474–1566). He became an advocate for their rights. When religious men such as Las Casas reported atrocities committed by Spanish soldiers against the natives to the Crown in Spain, they got results. King Ferdinand and Queen Isabella responded to the claims of Spanish abuse against the Native Americans by creating the Council of the Indies. It was the council's task to keep watch over the conduct of all Spanish soldiers. In 1513, the council issued the Laws of Burgos, which insisted that the conquistadors "treat the Indians with kindness."[8] When Spanish soldiers refused to obey the Laws of Burgos, the council drafted new laws that ended

Indian slavery and denied property rights for a soldier's heirs if they broke the law. Such men became the champions of the oppressed native peoples of Mexico and Central America. But men such as Las Casas were rare. Overall, the result of Spanish settlement in the New World was the same: The Native Americans suffered heartache and loss, while the Spanish colonists gained power and treasure.

CONQUERING EMPIRES

Because Columbus had landed first on an island in the Caribbean Sea, the Spanish began settling first on those islands. They established outpost settlements on Cuba, Puerto Rico, and Jamaica. Spanish explorers and soldiers used those island bases as springboards to fan out to new lands they wanted to conquer. In 1513, Juan Ponce de León led a party of Spanish soldiers and missionaries to modern-day Florida, which gave the Spanish claim to the lands that would one day become part of the southeastern United States. During that same year, Vasco Núñez de Balboa reached Central America (he had been a stowaway on a ship and was found too late to return him to Spain), where he followed Indian guides across the narrow strip of land called the Isthmus of Panama, reaching the Pacific Ocean, which he claimed in the name of his Spanish king. As these conquistadors and explorers searched for new lands, they usually took control of local natives. Sometimes, the control they gained came at a heavy price, especially when native warriors fought against the bearded invaders.

The conquest of American Indians by the Spanish was done largely by taking control of small tribal groups. There were many such groups, often living in small villages. These villages were home to only a few Indians, so a well-armed force of Spanish soldiers could easily defeat them. The Spanish conquistadors wore shiny, steel armor on their chests and gleaming helmets on their heads. They were skilled in the use of the sword, the lance, and the musket. They rode on horses, the first the Indians of the Americas had ever seen, which terrified them. And the soldiers used cannon that roared with each blast, sending out flames that the Native Americans thought was lightning. Terror was an effective Spanish weapon in subduing the natives.

However, some natives lived in larger communities, even in cities. During the 1520s, the Spanish faced the powerful Aztec Empire in what is now Mexico. In 1519, an army of 600 Spanish soldiers landed along the coast of eastern Mexico. Because the fleet of ships landed on Good Friday, "the day of the True Cross,"[9] the Spanish would name the site Veracruz, "the True Cross." They were led by a Spaniard from the province of Castile, a willful nobleman and military adventurer named Hernán Cortéz. He had heard stories of a great empire of Indians in Mexico, one fabulously rich with gold. He wanted to see the empire for himself and bring it under the control of the Spanish monarchy. From the coast, Cortéz and his men moved inland, meeting Indians along the way. They fought some of them while other Indians allied themselves with the Spaniards. This latter group hated the Aztecs who sometimes made them slaves, required them to pay tribute money, and even stole their relatives, killing them as human sacrifices. Such natives flocked to join Cortéz against the Aztecs. Eventually, perhaps as many as 200,000 Indians were allied with the Spaniards to fight against the Aztecs.

When Cortéz and his soldiers reached the Aztec capital of Tenochtitlán (now Mexico City), they found a modern city with streets, canals, massive stone buildings, and an empire that, unfortunately for the Aztecs, was divided. A power struggle was going on between rival groups within the Aztec Empire. When they reached Tenochtitlán, the Spanish found that the rumors of Aztec gold were indeed true. It appeared to be everywhere. It drove the Spanish invaders on as nothing else could. Cortéz himself described the allure gold had for his men, as well as

In 1519, Spanish conquistador Hernán Cortéz arrived in Mexico with 11 ships and an army of 600 soldiers. As Cortéz and his men moved inland, they encountered several Indian tribes, many of which chose to ally themselves with him in his quest to conquer the mighty Aztec Empire.

for himself: "I and my companions suffer from a disease of the heart which can be cured only with gold."[10] It was a "disease" that the Aztecs themselves noted about the Spanish. One Aztec eyewitness later wrote: "[The Spanish] picked up the gold and fingered it like monkeys. [They were] transported by joy, as if their hearts were illumined and made new."[11]

Cortéz began to methodically conquer the vast and advanced Aztec Empire. He appeared to be a god to the Aztecs. Cortéz rode on a horse and wore a full suit of steel armor. Once again, despite the size of the Aztec Empire, the armor-clad Spaniards managed to subdue their superstitious enemies with flaming guns and cannon. This took place in a short period of time even though the Spaniards had only 600 men. But, while weapons and allies were important in the fight to conquer the Aztecs, the Spanish had another weapon at their disposal—germs. As Cortéz's army marched across Mexico, one of the conquistador's men became infected with smallpox. Many of the Indians in the New World who came into contact with this disease became sick and died within a few days. Other diseases, such as measles, typhus, and influenza, were nearly as deadly. These diseases helped to weaken the Aztec Empire.

Within one year of Cortéz's landing on the coast of Mexico, nearly 40 percent of the Indian population living in central Mexico had died, just from smallpox alone. There was so much death that Aztec society and culture simply fell apart. As one survivor of smallpox wrote:

> The illness was so dreadful that no one could walk or move. The sick were so utterly helpless that they could only lie on their beds like corpses, unable to move their limbs or even their heads. . . . If they did move their bodies, they screamed with pain.[12]

On November 8, 1519, Hernán Cortéz and his troops entered the Aztec capital of Tenochtitlán (present-day Mexico City), where they encountered the leader of the Aztecs, Moctezuma. Believing Cortéz to be the incarnation of the Aztec god Quetzalcoatl, Moctezuma welcomed the Spanish and was thus an easy target for them to capture.

Over the following 80 years—to the end of the sixteenth century—the Indian population of Mexico was reduced from more than 15 million inhabitants to fewer than 1 million.

By 1521, the conquest of the Aztec Empire was complete. During the fighting, the Spanish had destroyed entire villages of Indians. They had managed to take the Aztec emperor, Moctezuma, prisoner. In time, they put him to death. Then, the emperor's successor died just three months later of yet another European disease. Chaos befell the Aztecs, brought by Spanish guns and steel, horses and germs. The greatest Indian empire in Central and North America had been brought down in less than two years. By the following decade, other Spanish conquistadors would bring about the defeat of yet another New World empire, this one far down in South America—the Incas.

CONQUERING YET ANOTHER NEW WORLD EMPIRE

The march of Spanish power in the Americas seemed to have no end. A decade following the conquest and collapse of the Aztec Empire, another vast empire was also destroyed by the Spanish. In 1532, another conquistador, Francisco Pizarro, brought down the vast kingdom of the Incas in South America.

The Inca Empire was gigantic, extending more than 2,000 miles from what is now Ecuador to Chile. It was the largest empire in all of the Americas. Just as with the Aztecs, the Spanish were lured south to the Inca Empire by stories of extraordinary riches and wealth. With 180 Spanish soldiers under his command, Pizarro was able to defeat the Incas. He arrived on their doorstep at the right time.

The Inca Empire had been divided by a civil war. The two sons of the former emperor, who had died of smallpox, were fighting one another when the Spaniards arrived in the Peruvian Andes, where the Incas lived. One of the sons, Atahualpa, had just managed to defeat his half brother, Huascar, and was headed to the northern part of the empire to take his place on the Incan throne in Cuzco, the capital. It was during his royal trip to the capital that Pizarro caught up with Atahualpa and took him prisoner. When the emperor offered to have his people pay a ransom for his release, Pizarro agreed. The Incas willingly filled an entire room with Incan treasure—gold, silver, and jewels—to free their leader. But after the ransom was paid, Pizarro ordered Atahualpa put to death by strangulation. Soon, the Spanish took control of Cuzco, gaining power over the entire Inca Empire. The Spanish established a new capital for themselves at Lima.

SPANISH POWER RISES TO
NEW HEIGHTS

Through the efforts of such bold, although ruthless, conquistadors as Cortéz and others, the Spanish were able to conquer lands throughout the Americas. Within 50 years of Columbus having reached the New World, Spanish royal power held sway over lands from the Caribbean to Mexico to the distant empire of the Incas in South America. The result was a new Spanish empire—New Spain—and its power seemed limitless.

The Spanish were tapping the riches of these vast American regions for themselves. They forced thousands of Native Americans to work for them. Great silver mines in Peru and Bolivia added daily to Spanish wealth in the Western Hemisphere. In the Caribbean, the Spanish found a new source of wealth, a white "gold" that grew tall in the fields—sugar. African slaves were imported in great numbers to work the sugar plantations. But the Spanish were not satisfied with their New World wealth or the extent of New Spain. They longed for more. Their endless desire for gold drove them to look to new places to spread Spanish influence, power, and control. They soon looked to North America, where they hoped there were more wealthy Indian empires. After all, stories of such places were being told in the streets of Mexico City.

3

Tales of Northern Gold

The Spanish conquest of the Aztec Empire was barely com-
pleted when the Spanish looked to North America for new
sources of wealth, as well as limitless lands to conquer. In 1513,
Ponce de León reached Florida, but the whole of North America
still lay open to Spanish exploration. Just five years after defeat-
ing the Aztecs, Cortéz wrote a letter to the king of Spain from
the capital of New Spain, Mexico City:

> I have a goodly number of people ready to go to settle at
> the Rio de las Palmas . . . because I have been informed that
> it is good land and that there is a port. I do not think God
> and Your majesty will be served less there than in all the
> other regions because I have much good news concerning
> that land.[13]

Cortéz's letter spoke of a river to the north—Rio de las Palmas. This was the river that would one day be called the Rio
Grande. This vast river cut through the lands that are today
part of the American Southwest and the modern-day states of

26

New Mexico and Texas. The mouth of the river had been explored more than once by Spanish adventurers and royal officials, who had determined it would be a good spot for a Spanish settlement. Such an outpost would have a port where Spanish ships could dock, and the river would provide a route for future Spanish explorers to move easily into the rugged frontier of North America. Cortéz's letter was favorably received by the Spanish monarch. Cortéz was able to secure a royal charter authorizing the creation of a colonial settlement at the mouth of the Rio de las Palmas.

But Cortéz would not remain involved in the unfolding plans to build this new Spanish colony to the north. Enemies in the king's court convinced the monarch that Cortéz was too ambitious. He should be removed from power, they told the king. Soon, Cortéz lost his office, and the new charter was handed off to another, a colonial leader ready to make a name for himself—Pánfilo de Narváez.

A COLONIZING FAILURE

In 1527, Narváez left his home in Spain and took passage on a ship bound for Cuba, the Spanish center of colonization in the Caribbean. There, Narváez gathered all the necessary provisions he would need to establish a successful colony at the mouth of the Rio de las Palmas. The Crown, it seems, did not want to spare any expense. He was provided with five ships, 600 male colonists, and at least 80 horses. Columbus had only been given three ships in his attempt to sail to Asia.

In April 1528, the flotilla set sail from Cuba and headed toward the Gulf Coast. Tragedy soon befell Narváez and his men. A great storm struck the fleet, and the colonizing party was blown far off course. At the site of modern-day Tampa Bay, one of his ships crashed onto the rocks and broke apart. Several of his other ships were seriously damaged. His plans in shambles,

Narváez made a decision to march approximately 300 of his men, nearly all his soldiers, across the Gulf Coast and reach the Rio de las Palmas by land. His remaining, yet damaged, four ships were to sail ahead, with their crews. They would all meet up later at the mouth of the Rio de las Palmas, soldiers and sailors alike.

The situation did not improve for the Narváez expedition. The ships accidentally sailed past the mouth of the Rio de las Palmas and became lost. The small fleet spent the greater part of a year sailing back and forth across the Gulf, from Texas to Florida, looking for Narváez and his men. They finally abandoned the effort, sailing south to Veracruz, hoping to hear some good news about the fate of Narváez and his men. No one in the port knew anything about the lost party of would-be colonizers.

As for Narváez and his men, they were also facing difficulties. After months of straggling along, with 50 of his men having died, Narváez and his remaining soldiers decided to try their luck at sea. They built small, simple boats covered with horsehide, intent on riding the Gulf currents south to Mexico. For weeks, they struggled to maneuver these boats beyond the coastal currents and into open water. Finally, near the mouth of the Mississippi River, another violent storm rolled in and thrust them out to sea and out of sight of one another. Many of them perished, including Narváez. Only about 80 men survived and were washed up on the shores of Texas. Some of them landed along Galveston Bay. One of them was the man who had been appointed to serve as the Rio de las Palmas colony's treasurer and high sheriff—Álvar Nuñez Cabeza de Vaca. After a grueling eight years spent lost and wandering in the deserts of the modern-day American Southwest, Cabeza de Vaca and a handful of other survivors were picked up by Spanish soldiers on patrol in northern Mexico. When the men were returned to Mexico City, Cabeza de Vaca told the viceroy of tales he had heard of great

Despite encountering hardship during his eight-year trek across the barren lands of the American Southwest, Álvar Núñez Cabeza de Vaca was convinced that there was a land of unbelievable riches just beyond the region he wandered through. Cabeza de Vaca recounted these tales in what became known as *Naufragios*, or *Shipwrecks*.

riches in the lands to the north. It did not take long before the viceroy of New Spain was ready to send a conquistador into the region in search of gold and Spanish glory.

THE LURE OF GOLDEN RICHES

With the return of Álvar Nuñez Cabeza de Vaca to Mexico City, Spanish eyes turned to the lands he had wandered across for eight years—today's American Southwest. His curiosity piqued by Cabeza de Vaca's stories about cities of gold, the viceroy of New Spain, Antonio de Mendoza, launched a mission in search of new colonies and treasure. The young hidalgo Francisco Vásquez de Coronado would serve nicely as leader. He had been brought to America by Viceroy Mendoza. He would do anything the Spanish high official told him to do.

To encourage Coronado, Mendoza made him a governor of the lands to the north of Mexico—New Galicia. The young aristocrat would be exploring territory that was his to rule. But before dispatching Coronado, Mendoza decided to send a well-known Franciscan friar into the region. (He was known for having written a report that criticized the treatment of the Incas by Pizarro and his soldiers.) Coronado may have been willing to play the role of the explorer, but Father Marcos de Niza already was one. He had been on other explorations, to Peru and Central America. He had proven himself fearless. The padre was also an excellent mapmaker. He was to study the land, its trees, plants, animals, rivers, mineral wealth, and people. Was the region to the north well populated? What were the natives like? Were their villages large or small? To help Father Marcos on his scouting mission into the northlands, he was provided with a guide, one who had traveled through the region himself. He was the Moor who had accompanied Cabeza de Vaca and his Spanish comrades—Esteban.

On March 7, 1539, Father Marcos, Esteban, and hundreds of Indians set out to the north. (Another friar, Father Honorato, also set out with the party, but became ill and had to drop out of the expedition.) Once underway, Father Marcos began having doubts about his Moorish companion. Esteban thought he was extremely important to the mission and acted as if everything depended on him. He wanted the Indians they contacted to think he was a medicine man or someone with magical powers so he "[wore] bells on his ankles and elbows and [carried] a gourd rattle decorated with feathers," much the same as Indian healers.[14] He dressed in brightly colored robes and wore a plumed headdress. Father Marcos decided to separate himself from Esteban.

He told the Moor to move ahead of him by a few miles. Esteban was to send runners back to report to the padre when he reached an Indian settlement. Esteban signaled the size of each village by having his Indian messengers carry crosses back to the friar. The larger the cross, the bigger the village.

THE MOOR AND THE FRIAR

During the first three months of exploring, the stories Esteban sent back to the Franciscan holy man were exciting, indeed. There were reports of the Seven Cities. There were even reports of greater cities farther north in the distant provinces—the kingdoms of Totonteac, Acus, and Marata. By May, after two months of travel through the remote lands of the Sonora Valley, the party entered a great desert that led them out of northern Mexico and into a mysterious land that is today New Mexico, where Santa Fe would one day be built. Food became scarce in the scrublands. The Spaniards and their Indian comrades ate rabbits and other small animals.

Because Father Marcos had decided that Esteban should move ahead of him, the Moor came to believe this was a sign of his personal importance. He began to act proudly and ex-pected the Indians he encountered to honor him. In each vil-lage, Esteban wanted to be treated like a god, expecting gifts of turquoise, as well as young women. When Esteban reached the Zuni Indian village of Hawikuh, he sent an Indian runner back to the priest with a cross as large as he was. Hawikuh was a large and important village. But it would be the last Esteban visited. When he entered the town of the Zunis, he demanded they give him women for his pleasure. Because the Zunis protected their women closely, they chose, instead, to kill Esteban, as well as many of his Indian escorts.

This news was sent back to Father Marcos by the only two Indians who survived the massacre of Esteban and his com-rades. Before his death, Esteban sent word back to the father several times, informing him that the Indians he spoke to told him of "seven very great cities, all under one lord" with "houses of stone and lime . . . very large."[15] Esteban's messages to the padre became more and more detailed. As Father Marcos later wrote: "Many other particulars he told me of these seven cities, as well as of other provinces farther away, each of which, he said, was greater than the seven cities."[16] But with Esteban dead, the padre decided to turn back and report to

FATHER MARCOS'S REPORT: FACT OR FICTION?

When Viceroy Mendoza sent Father Marcos into the lands north of New Spain (present-day New Mexico) in the spring of 1539, he told him to gather as much information about the land and its people as he could. But Mendoza made it clear to the Franciscan padre that he was most interested in the legend of the Seven Cities of Gold that Cabeza de Vaca and Esteban had described after their eight-year journey through the region.

After exploring the northlands for several months, Father Marcos had returned to Mexico City with a glowing report. The Seven Cities were real. The wealth of the north was fabulous. The words greatly excited the viceroy and led him to send Coronado into the region on a military expedition.

But was the Franciscan father telling the truth? The answer may be complicated. Because the padre had decided to send Esteban ahead of him to meet with the local Indians, much of what he learned was reported to him secondhand. He was often given information about things that he did not see for himself. Stories about riches and gold were exactly what the padre wanted to hear, so was he told the truth? It is difficult to know.

It is known, however, that the Franciscan explorer did make several claims of his own concerning the sites he had seen in the northlands. For example, he told the viceroy that he had seen an impressive Indian settlement, a "very beautiful city . . . bigger than the city of Mexico . . . situated on the brow of a roundish hill."* Father Marcos called it one of the Seven Cities of Cíbola.

his viceroy. He did manage to take time to build up a pile of stones and mount them with a large cross. He did this "in the name of Don Antonio de Mendoza, viceroy of New Spain, for the Emperor, our lord, in token possession of all the seven cities."[17]

Even as Father Marcos made his way back to Mexico City, he spotted Indian "cities" in the distance. He would later claim to have met with local Indians who told him about the towns

The town he described was the Zuni village of Hawikuh, where Esteban had been killed. But had Father Marcos even seen the city he described as larger than Mexico City? Today, historians doubt his claim. According to his own report, the padre "had not allowed enough time to travel the full distance to Hawikuh from where he said he had been encamped when the messengers arrived."** Also, Hawikuh was not on a "roundish hill," but on top of a flat mesa. If he saw it himself, he grossly exaggerated its size, because it was only one-sixtieth the size of Mexico City. It appears that the excitable Father Marcos chose to tell Viceroy Mendoza more than he had actually seen with his own eyes.

There are other indications that the Franciscan stretched the truth. According to one of the padre's own servants, Father Marcos described the Seven Cities of Cíbola as follows: "The cities were surrounded with walls, with their gates guarded, and were very wealthy, having silversmiths; and that the women wore strings of gold beads and the men girdles of gold and white woolen dresses; and that they had sheep and cows and partridges and slaughterhouses and iron forges."*** There is no evidence that the Indians of the region of the Southwest lived in cities of great wealth or that any of the rest of Father Marcos's colorful descriptions were true.

* Lynn I. Perrigo, *The American Southwest: Its People and Cultures* (Albuquerque: University of New Mexico Press, 1971), 22.
** Ibid.
*** George Daniels, ed. *The Spanish West* (New York: Time-Life Books, 1976), 29.

he saw along the way. "I was informed," he said, that these cities held "much gold, and that the natives . . . trade in vessels and jewels for the ears, and little plates with which they scrape themselves and remove the sweat."[18] By the time Father Marcos returned to Mexico City, he had many stories to tell of the lands, the people, and the fabulous cities he had seen for himself throughout the northern lands.

Viceroy Mendoza listened with eager attention to Father Marcos, just as he had to Cabeza de Vaca after his return. The Franciscan padre told him of the death of Esteban and of nearly all his Indian escorts. He described the Indians responsible as hostile to the party of explorers. He went on to describe in rich detail the lands he had crossed. The Seven Cities of Gold were there, he claimed. The natives had told of its wealth over and over. The viceroy could not have been more excited. He rewarded Father Marcos with a new job. He appointed him head of all the Franciscan brothers of Mexico. Mendoza would now send a full expeditionary force into the northern lands under Coronado's leadership.

CORONADO LEADS AN EXPEDITION

When word spread of a grand expedition, one involving soldiers and priests, Spaniards flocked to join. Some of those who volunteered were, like Coronado, hidalgos of noble birth. Others were "vicious young men with nothing to do."[19] Coronado interviewed each one of them until he had amassed an army of 300 soldiers. Among their number, 240 were cavalrymen and 60 were foot soldiers. They were accompanied by 800 Indians, "armed with spears, bows and huge wooden swords edged with shards of flint or volcanic glass."[20] Viceroy Mendoza gave orders to Coronado on January 6, 1540. He was to march north in search of the Seven Cities of Cíbola. By Sunday, February 22, the entire party was assembled at a site

In February 1540, Francisco Vázquez de Coronado and 300 Spaniards traveled north from Mexico City in search of the Seven Cities of Cíbola. Over the next two years, Coronado and his men ventured all the way to present-day Kansas but found little more than scattered Indian villages along their journey.

along the Pacific Coast. It was a grand occasion in Spanish colonial history. Nearly half a century following Columbus's arrival in the New World, the Spanish were preparing to extend, by force if necessary, their control over yet another region of the Americas. As they set out for points unknown, Coronado and his men marched and rode past the viceroy as he reviewed the expedition:

It was the most brilliant review ever held in the New World. The cavaliers wore shining armor and were mounted on splendid horses equipped with colored blankets, leather armor, and silver-mounted harness; each foot soldier was armed with crossbow and harquebus [a type of heavy

36   SANTA FE

gun], sword and shield; and the Indians were splashed with warpaint and decked in multicolored plumage.[21]

The party also included several friars. Among them was Father Marcos. Accompanying the soldiers, Indians, and other members of the expedition were herds of animals. The Coronado expedition was "intended to be the best-fed party that had so far entered the Southwest."[22] There were sheep, goats, pigs, and cattle, all on the hoof, their purpose to provide food, including milk and meat.

The day following the grand review before the viceroy, Coronado and his men prepared to head north. Priests performed a Mass, then Viceroy Mendoza spoke to the assembled men, telling them they were to obey Coronado and that great rewards lay ahead for all of them. The soldiers were paid 30 pesos, but it was the promise of land grants that motivated most of them. On February 23, Coronado gave the order for his massive expedition to begin its march.

4

Coronado's March

Although much preparation had gone into the planning of the great march of Francisco Vásquez de Coronado, the expedition did not go well from the beginning. The whole party moved slowly along, and traversing mountain passes was difficult. The horses struggled through the tablelands, broad, level, elevated areas of the terrain, and animals wandered away from their herds. While herders went out to round up strays, Coronado and his soldiers had to stop and wait. The slow progress of his party was something Coronado could not accept. Approximately five weeks after his party began its march, the leader of the expedition decided he needed to move faster than his main party was capable of. He decided to leave them behind, while he and a handpicked unit of 100 troops, including 75 cavalrymen and 25 foot soldiers, sped forward. These men were also accompanied by Father Marcos, along with three other Franciscan friars. To make certain his advance scouting unit could travel light, Coronado ordered them to take along only one pound of personal items. These front troops took no animals and were to live on minimal field rations.

DOUBTS ABOUT THE FRIAR

By this time, Coronado and many of his men had serious doubts about Father Marcos and his earlier reports of Cíbola and its wealth. The party had met up, after traveling 200 miles, with some Spanish scouts that had been sent ahead four months earlier, before Coronado and his men left in late February. Their report was not good. Their leader, Melchior Diaz, appeared before them nearly starved and exhausted. He and his small party had survived the harsh winter of 1539–40, and some of his Indian scouts had died because of the cold. He told Coronado of the local Indians he had met to the north and reported he had seen no gold or other sources of vast wealth. It appears they did have much turquoise, but, Diaz noted, "not so [much] as the father provincial [Marcos] said."[23] Nor had Diaz found any of the great cities that the Franciscan priest had told Viceroy Mendoza about. Diaz also delivered other bad news. He had received a message from some of the Indians he had encountered that informed him that they would kill any Spaniard who tried to cross their lands. Such reports were hardly comforting. Many of the facts told by Diaz did not match up with those told earlier by Father Marcos. Early in the Coronado expedition, the Spaniards began to question whether Father Marcos had actually seen all he had claimed.

As Coronado advanced with his own scouting force, he followed the west coast of Mexico for the first 200 miles or so. This region was the Sonora Valley, where the land was fertile, watered by many rivers that crossed the Spaniard's path. In time, the party reached the lands that would one day be Arizona. There, the land was barren, water became more difficult to find, and living off the land was nearly impossible. When the advance party arrived along the San Pedro River, they soon reached an Indian village that Father Marcos had described in his earlier report—Chichilticalli. While the Franciscan priest had described the

On the advice of Father Marcos de Niza, who promised Francisco
Vásquez de Coronado that his expedition would come across a city of
vast riches, Coronado and his troops reached the town of Hawikuh
(in present-day New Mexico) in July 1540. Although the Spanish did
not enter the town, they demanded that the town's residents lay down
their weapons and submit. The ensuing conflict is depicted in this
painting by sixteenth-century Dutch artist Jan Mostaert.

town as large and active with trade, it was tiny, no more than "a
single miserable hovel, made of red earth and lacking a roof."[24]

Coronado and his advance party were already experiencing
the heat of that summer. It was June, and the conditions became
miserable for man and animal alike. There was almost no food
and no villages where the Spaniards might be able to trade. Some
of the party's horses collapsed, dying of exhaustion and a lack
of food and water. When one of the soldiers, along with several
of the party's Indian guides, ate some type of local weed, they,
too, died. For 150 miles, Coronado and his small scouting party
struggled through the harsh Arizona desert. Then, fortunately,
they reached the Gila River, where they found grass for their

horses. Soon, on July 6, they reached the Zuni Valley of modern-day New Mexico. Coronado and his men had covered 1,000 miles since they had set out more than four months earlier.

Here, the Spanish party approached the first of the cities that Father Marcos had described as those of Cíbola—Hawikuh. After passing through an inhospitable desert, the men were ready to enjoy the riches of the first of the seven cities of great wealth. But their dreams of gold were soon dashed:

> Here were no stately walls, no turquoise-studded portals, no silversmith shops, no sign of wealth. True, some of the houses were multistoried, as Fray [Father] Marcos had reported; but otherwise the alleged metropolis fell hopelessly short of Fray Marcos' favorable comparison to Mexico City. . . . The Spaniards judged it to hold perhaps 800 people.[25]

The soldiers immediately turned on Father Marcos in anger. The man who served as Coronado's historian on the expedition wrote: "Such were the curses that some hurled at him that I pray God may protect him from them."[26]

THE ZUNIS REACT

Although the Spaniards had reached the town of Hawikuh, they did not immediately enter it. Coronado remained cautious, especially when a band of local Indians, the Zunis, emerged from the town ready to fight. The conquistador leader sent some of the priests and Indian interpreters to speak to the Zunis. They were to read an official statement to them known as the Requirement of 1513. This royal document had been drawn up years earlier to read to Indians the Spanish encountered on any of their expeditions. The "Requirement" opened with a brief history of the world, the Catholic Church, and the Kingdom of Spain. Then, it "continued with a demand that the Indians yield themselves to the Spanish Crown and accept the preaching of Christianity."[27] The Requirement of 1513 went on to explain that if the Indians accepted Spanish rule and the Catholic faith, they would become subjects and not be attacked. But if they did not agree, "we shall take away your goods, and shall do all the harm and damage that we can, as to vassals that do not obey."[28] Indians hearing these words for the first time could not truly understand them. It had become practice within the Spanish Empire that following such a reading conquistadors would usually attack.

This encounter between Coronado's advance party and the Zunis turned out the same. The Zunis, uncertain of the strangers before them, launched a shower of arrows at the Spaniards. The soldiers then shouted the name "Santiago," and advanced against their attackers. ("Santiago" referred to St. James, the Spanish patron saint of soldiers.) A dozen Zunis were felled by Spanish guns and swords. The Indian warriors scurried up ladders to the roofs of their pueblos for protection. The Spaniards were not far behind them. The battle unfolded with the Zunis firing their arrows down at Coronado's men. The fighting caught Coronado's men at their weakest. They had just emerged hungry and tired from their long march across the desert. The fight was not easy for them: "The crossbowmen soon broke the strings of their crossbows and the musketeers could no nothing, because they had arrived so weak and feeble that they could scarcely stand on their feet."[29]

As for Coronado, he was in the midst of the battle. The Zunis quickly figured out he was the leader of the invaders now besieging their homes: "Coronado's gilded armor marked him as a special target. Rocks and arrows clanged against his helmet and cuirass [upper-body armor]. Finally, a boulder knocked him from the ladder. He crashed to the ground and lay there unconscious."[30] With their leader injured, Spanish soldiers rushed to help him. Coronado was dragged from the fighting (some thought he was dead) and placed in a tent away from the battle where "he remained unconscious for a long time."[31]

Once Coronado came to, the fight was over. He was informed that his men had fought on and continued to press the

THE ZUNI INDIANS

One of the first tribal groups of American Indians that Coronado and his men made contact with and fought were the Zuni Indians. Their ancestors had lived in the region for hundreds of years before the arrival of the Spanish.

The name *Zuni* (pronounced "Zoon-YE" or "Zoon-EE") comes from the Spanish. It was their name for the people and the pueblo where they lived. Their original name was *Ashiwi*, which has been translated several ways, including "the flesh." This tribal and cultural group lived primarily in six pueblo villages along the northern banks of the upper Zuni River, in western modern-day New Mexico. They have lived there for approximately 800 years. Today, the Zunis live in the same basic locations they were occupying when Coronado and his party arrived in the 1540s. At that time, the Zunis may have numbered as many as 20,000.

The ancient ancestors of the more modern Zunis were the peoples known today as the Mogollon and the Anasazi. They were also descended from Mexican Indians who have called the Southwest their home as far back as 2,000 years ago. By the eleventh century, the Zuni peoples had erected their "village of the great kiva," near the later town of Zuni. By the 1300s and 1400s, the Zuni Valley was home to a large number of villages. Following the arrival of the Spanish, their numbers declined. By 1650, only six Zuni villages were still occupied.

The Zuni villages were, as they are today, multistoried houses called pueblos. The Indian men built these homes of stone and plaster, not of adobe bricks, which were commonly used on pueblos farther east. The Zuni pueblos did not have doors to provide protection against invaders. Those living in the pueblos entered their homes by scaling ladders and climbing down through the roofs.

For most of their history, the Zunis have worked their surrounding fields as farmers, growing several varieties of corn (maize), as well as beans, squash, and cotton. After the arrival of the Spanish, the Zunis began raising wheat,

Zunis. Protected by their armor, the Spaniards had climbed the pueblo ladders and fought the Indians on rooftops and in the streets. The fighting had not lasted more than an hour. The Zuni warriors had finally surrendered, begging their enemies "not to hurt them any more, as they wished to leave the pueblo."[32]

chilies, oats, and a new type of fruit—peaches. Zuni women ground the corn into flour and worked it into breads. Also, men provided food by hunting, while women gathered wild plants, such as berries, roots, and pinyon nuts.

Today, approximately 7,000 Indians live in the Zuni pueblos. One of the most important economic activities at Zuni Pueblo is the manufacture of turquoise and silver jewelry. Although the Zunis encountered by Coronado were already turquoise craftsmen, the art form was further developed as one of the most unique aspects of modern Zuni culture.

Today the Zunis live in the same region—west-central New Mexico—that they inhabited nearly six centuries ago. Traditionally, the Zunis lived in six villages, including Zuni, which is pictured here in 1903.

The casualties among the Spanish were not high. They included 10 or 12 wounded or hurt soldiers, plus Coronado, whose wounds were quite extensive. He had two sharp cuts on his face and was bruised from head to toe. An arrow had pierced his foot, where it had lodged. He had been hit with many rocks. One had struck him so sharply that his helmet was badly dented. But he had survived. Three horses also were killed.

With the defeat of the Zunis, the Spanish began to take inventory of the town they had fought to conquer. Although they found no gold of note, they found something else that was more important to them at that moment, tired and hungry as they were. As one conquistador described things: "There we found something we prized more than gold or silver, namely, much maize, beans, and chickens larger than those here of New Spain, and salt better and whiter than I have ever seen in my whole life."[33]

The battle with the Zunis and the taking of Hawikuh gave the Spanish a clearer picture of the world they had entered with such excitement and dreams of great riches. Almost nothing was as Father Marcos had described. Coronado, in his first report after the battle, had little good to say about the Franciscan padre. "Not to be too verbose," the Spanish military leader wrote to Viceroy Mendoza, "I can assure you that [Father Marcos] has not told the truth in a single thing he said, but everything is the opposite of what he related, except that name of the cities and the large stone houses."[34] He explained that the "Seven Cities are seven little villages, all within a radius of five leagues."[35] Coronado was too angry and disappointed with the father to allow him to remain in his party. Once he finished his report, he sent it back to Mexico City on August 3, along with Father Marcos. His messengers were to contact the larger force that had been following Coronado and give them the news of the battle and the conquest.

During the weeks that followed the battle at Hawikuh, Coronado's advance party brought the other pueblos in the region under Spanish control. The Seven Cities of Cíbola were easily captured, but they were not islands of wealth in the midst of a great desert in the Southwest. The men did recover physically after their grueling march, eating the Zunis' food. As they encountered more and more Indians in the region, they began to hear stories, tales they had heard first from Father Marcos. The riches of Cíbola lay farther north. The gold they sought was beyond their villages, north over the desert mountains.

5

Coronado Continues His Expedition

Even as the Spaniards discovered they had been misled about the wealth of the Indians they would come to know as the Zuni, they did not give up hope. New rumors pointed farther north. Coronado wasted little time planning his next expedition. While most of his scouting party waited for the main expeditionary force to catch up to them, he sent 20 soldiers ahead in search of the elusive riches. (Coronado's wounds were too severe to allow him to go along with them.) Making good time, the new scouting party reached the villages of the Hopi Indians after covering 75 miles of desert territory. Here, as at Hawikuh, there was no gold of consequence. The soldiers reported back to Coronado, telling their leader of a new discovery—a major river flowing north of where the Hopis lived off toward the west. The Spanish leader soon sent another small party to investigate, under the command of Garcia López de Cárdenas. Cárdenas and his men reached the village of the Hopis, picked up food supplies, and continued on in the company of Hopi guides.

In September 1540, during their search for the Colorado River, Captain Garcia López de Cárdenas and a group of Spanish soldiers encountered a breathtaking site: a great chasm that dropped several thousand feet to the river below. A group of Hopi Indians had led them to what is today known as the Grand Canyon.

A GRAND DISCOVERY

Three weeks later, having crossed a desolate desert, the Spaniards reached the great river of rumor. It lay at the bottom of a vast canyon. The canyon was so immense, the Spanish soldiers could not believe their eyes. As they stood on a rock rim above

the canyon, the newly arrived Europeans could see a thin rib-
bon of ruddy water flowing between the canyon walls that stood
taller than a modern skyscraper. It was the Colorado River. The
great chasm that spread out before them would later be named
the Grand Canyon. For three days, the Spaniards remained at
the canyon, exploring, searching for a pathway down to the river. When three members of the party finally found a way down,
they descended until the remainder of the party lost them from
their sight.

Even as the curious Spaniards took in the spectacle of the
Grand Canyon, Coronado was visited by Indians who had
heard about the Spanish. They came from another pueblo town,
Cicuye, several hundred miles farther east. The Indians were the
Tiguex. They came in peace, they explained in sign language,
and they gave permission to the Spaniards to travel across their
lands. Coronado told them he would do so soon. He selected a
party of 20 soldiers, led by Hernando de Alvarado, to accompa-
ny the Tiguex back to their village. On August 29, the Spaniards
and Tiguex headed east and, just five days later, reached another
pueblo complex. Father Marcos had described it in his report,
calling it Acus. The pueblo sat atop a mesa called Acoma. When
the Spaniards approached the pueblo, the local Indians came
out and threatened to attack. But, it was probably only a test, for
when the Spaniards appeared to stand their ground, the Indians
gave them food and other gifts, including turkeys. Alvarado and
his men continued on.

By September 7, the party of Spaniards reached the Tiguex
Pueblo complex. Its buildings sat on both sides of the Rio
Grande. This was the Rio de las Palmas, the river to which Pán-
filo de Narváez had been sent to build a colony at its mouth. This
Spanish party was far inland and upriver from the Texas coast.
The residents of the village again proved friendly. Alvarado was
so impressed by them, that he sent word back to Coronado that

it would be a good place to set up his camp through the coming winter. However, the Spaniards pushed on. The next few days took the Spaniards up the Rio Grande, then to the Pecos River to the east. Soon, Alvarado and his men reached Cicuye, the home of the party of Tiguex Indians that had visited Coronado earlier. The Spaniards were impressed with the size of the pueblo, as one noted: "Its houses are four and five stories high, some of them being very fine. These people neither plant cotton nor raise turkeys because it is close to the plains where the cattle roam."[36] Alvarado was about to see, for the first time, the great American bison—the buffalo.

He set out with his men toward the east, along with a new guide. The local Indians had captured a Pawnee warrior who was from the Great Plains, far to the east. He was to lead Alvarado to the land of the buffalo. The Spaniards called the Pawnee warrior *El Turco*—the Turk—because, to them, "he looked like one."[37] With the Turk in the lead, Alvarado and his men soon crossed the Pecos River, then the Canadian River. Soon, the Spaniards saw their first buffalo herd, which one of Alvarado's men described as "the most monstrous beasts ever seen or read about."[38] Unfamiliar with these large animals, the Spaniards got a little too close and the buffalo charged, killing some of their horses. The soldiers did manage to kill some buffalo and enjoyed the taste of the meat. It was the first time Europeans had engaged in a buffalo hunt in what is now the American West.

But buffalo were not the only new sites the Turk offered to lead the Spaniards to see. He told them of a great distant city, which he called Quivira. He described in detail how Quivira was a land rich "with gold, silver and fabrics, and abundant and fruitful in everything."[39] Alvarado was not sure he believed the Turk's story. In order to convince Alvarado, the Turk claimed he had a gold bracelet he had received from the Indians at Quivira, but that it had been taken from him by the natives at Cicuye.

The Spanish leader then called his guide's bluff. He would take the Turk back to the Indian village and have them show him the bracelet.

NEW SETBACKS FOR CORONADO

Back at the Zuni village of Hawikuh, Coronado had finally recovered enough from his wounds to begin marching with his men. He had decided, after hearing from Alvarado, that he would take up winter quarters at Tiguex. Coronado then dispatched Cárdenas, who had returned from the Grand Canyon, to go ahead and begin preparing Tiguex for the larger army that was still straggling behind Coronado. Then, the situation deteriorated for the Spanish. Coronado met up with Alvarado, who had returned to Cicuye, and asked the local chiefs about the gold bracelet the Turk claimed they had taken from him. They said they knew nothing about the bracelet. When Alvarado decided they were lying, he took the chiefs as his prisoners. A pair of dogs were allowed to attack the chiefs to scare them into telling the Spaniards about the bracelet, but they still claimed they knew nothing about the Turk's claim. Meanwhile, Cárdenas had already ordered the Indians at Tiguex to leave their homes for the winter to make room for the Spanish. This had angered the Tiguex, especially because they had also been ordered to leave their winter supply of food in their pueblos for the Spanish. Both Coronado's captains had made serious errors in judgment. The local Indians were beginning to turn on the Spanish.

Everything began to fall apart shortly thereafter. One of Cárdenas's men attacked a beautiful Indian woman and raped her. (As he did so, he ordered her husband to hold the reins of his horse.) Word of the attack by the dogs on the chiefs and the sexual assault soon spread through the region from pueblo to pueblo. An attack took place at a Spanish horse corral, where

Many of the Native American villages the Spanish came across in the American Southwest had kivas, which are circular, sunken ceremonial chambers. Pictured here is a reconstruction of a kiva in the pueblo of Tiguex, which Francisco Vásquez de Coronado attacked in 1541.

the Tiguex killed an Indian guarding some of Coronado's horses. Thirty horses and mules were allowed to escape. Some of Cárdenas's men tracked down the Tiguex raiders who were hiding in a *kiva*, a circular, sunken ceremonial chamber. Two hundred Indians were captured and burned at the stake. Whether Coronado or Cárdenas gave the orders is uncertain. The massacre would be the last straw for the Pueblo Indians in the region. They were now prepared to fight the Spanish in an all-out war. The twelve pueblos of Tiguex were ready to shed the blood of Coronado's men.

Fortunately for Coronado, his main force had finally caught up with him. But their numbers had been reduced, with approximately one-fourth of his soldiers and Indian allies having died or been sent in small groups to deliver messages to Mexico City. He was facing 5,000 Tiguex Pueblo Indians. Coronado first targeted Moho, one of the Pueblo settlements. But, when he sent Cárdenas with a force of soldiers, the Tiguex surprised him, taking him prisoner. Only a desperate attack by Cárdenas's men freed their captain. The Spaniards then retreated. Coronado was furious. He set out with his entire military force to lay siege to Moho Pueblo.

A SIEGE AGAINST THE PUEBLO

The siege began in early January 1541. Coronado was determined to force the Indians to surrender. But the siege was to drag on for weeks. The Indians of Moho—approximately 400 in all, including women and children—had plenty of food. Their biggest problem was lack of water. The pueblo had only one well and it would not provide enough water for all the Indians. The future looked bleak for the residents of Moho Pueblo. But snows began to fall, giving the Indians the break they needed.

Coronado's siege dragged on until mid-March. Then, the Indians asked that some of their women and children be freed from the pueblo so they could survive. The Spanish agreed, letting about 100 women out. Many Indian women, however, chose to stay inside the pueblo with the men. When the pueblo's well dried up two weeks later, the Indians decided to break out. They first burned all their possessions, so they would leave nothing for the Spanish. In the middle of the night, the Tiguex tried to sneak out, only to have the Spanish discover them. A massacre then took place. Many Indians— including men, women, and children—were killed and most of the rest taken prisoner. Some managed to get away and cross the icy waters of the Rio Grande. But they did not make it to safety, many dying of wounds, while others froze to death. All told, 200 Pueblo Indians died, bringing Coronado's siege to a successful end.

ON TO QUIVIRA

The siege was a success for Coronado, because it not only brought an end to a single act of Indian defiance against the Spanish, but it ended Indian resistance in general. The Spanish had taught the Indians in the region a powerful lesson. The Tiguex may have had more warriors than the Spanish had, but the Spaniards had better weapons and were protected by their armor. There would be no more resistance. All the Peublo tribes accepted Spanish control.

This freed Coronado to continue his explorations. The legend of Quivira and its riches continued to lead the Spanish farther east. It was spring, and Coronado could expect fair weather for his men during their journey. The Turk still spoke of the distant riches of this mysterious land, where there "was so much gold . . . that they could load not only horses with it but wagons."[40] He told how Quivira was a place where everyone ate their food, even the most unimportant people, off silver plates and drank out of golden goblets. A giant canoe with 40 oars of gold delivered Quivira's king up and down a river that stretched five miles across. The Turk even told of another land, beyond Quivira, called Harahey, which he said was even more fabulously wealthy. (He neglected to mention that Harahey was where his people, the Pawnee Indians, lived.)

In April 1541, Coronado set out with his men toward Quivira. To make certain that the residents of the pueblos of Tiguex remained subdued, the Spanish leader took along a large number of its people with him. It was a massive group that set out across the scrub desert of modern-day New Mexico. Between the Spanish, their loyal Indians allies, and their Tiguex captives, the party numbered more than 1,500 men, accompanied by

1,000 horses and mules. These pack animals carried huge supplies of food, mostly corn, enough to feed the entire expedition for more than a month. By the last week of April, Coronado led his party to the north along the Rio Grande, then turned toward the east at the Pecos River to Cicuye. There, the Spanish leader returned the two chiefs who had been kidnapped by Alvarado. This seemed to help ease the tension between the Cicuyans and the Spaniards. But the chiefs were still angry about the way they had been treated. They had told the Turk to lead the Spaniards on a long journey across the barren plains to the east, one that would take them too far away from the lands they had come from to ever return.

By early May, the Turk had led the Spaniards out onto the Great Plains. The traveling band saw buffalo herds that were so large that Coronado wrote "it would be impossible to estimate their number."[41] The expedition that was in search of Quivira had reached what is now Texas. Here, they soon encountered a new Indian tribe who called themselves the Querechos. They were nomadic buffalo hunters, who lived in tepees. They appeared, to Coronado, to be the healthiest Indians he had ever encountered. They did not fight the Spanish, and they even acted friendly. They were the Indians known today as the Apaches. The Apaches gave the Spanish directions that led them to the north across the panhandle of Texas.

However, there were problems for the expedition. They encountered bad weather, struggling through a tornado accompanied by large hailstones as large as a man's fist, which destroyed their encampments and pummeled the men, leaving their helmets dented. But the party pushed on. They came in contact with other Indians, the Tewas, who told them of a great village to the north. The Spanish did not seem to be getting any closer to the elusive wealth of Quivira, but they continued their journey, having already traveled 600 miles. The

During their exploration of what are today the plains of Texas, Oklahoma, and Kansas, the Spanish encountered an animal they had never seen before—the buffalo. In the sixteenth century, millions of buffalo roamed the plains and they were a valuable resource for most Native American tribes of the region.

Spaniards were confused, however, about the descriptions the Tewas gave of Quivira. These Indians told Coronado that Quivira did not have great wealth, and described a humble village, where the houses were made of "grass and hide . . . not of stone and several stories high."[42]

Coronado was growing impatient with all the stories of Quivira. His expeditionary force was, once again, moving too slow. In late May, he decided to march ahead of his main column with a handpicked force to reach Quivira as quickly as possible. The Spanish leader selected 30 superior horsemen, 6 proven foot soldiers, and a priest, Father Juan de Padilla. Believing that the Turk had his own motives for leading the Spanish toward the grassy plains to the north, Coronado had him placed in chains so he would not escape. Coronado left instructions to his main force that they were to wait eight days. If he did not return by then, they were to turn back and make their way to Tiguex. Once again Coronado pressed on.

ACROSS THE "STAKED PLAINS"

Through June, the Spaniards pushed across the Texas Panhandle and beyond, crossing territory that would be remembered as the *Llano Estacado*—the Staked Plains. (One story explaining the name is that Coronado's men placed small wooden stakes in the ground along the way to mark the route they were taking so they could find their way back. This story, however, has never been proven.) Then, they passed onto the flat plains country. Here the men lost perspective. There were no mountains, hills, mesas, or sandstone monuments to help them keep their positions fixed. Some of them wandered off while out hunting and did not return, "not knowing how to get back to where they started from."[43] On they went, into July, with its blazing heat. They crossed the Brazos and Red rivers, then marched into modern-day Oklahoma, crossed the Arkansas River, and continued north into Kansas. There, at last, they found the first of the villages of Quivira. It was not as the Turk had described, but everything the Tewas had said it would be. Quivira was a disappointing village of simple grass huts, "yapping dogs, naked children, shy women and a few men in primitive ceremonial regalia."[44] There was no gold, only poverty, but Coronado claimed the lands in the name of his king.

Over the next three weeks, the Spaniards continued their search, reaching one poor Indian village after another. (Historians believe Coronado traveled as far onto the Great Plains as the sites where Wichita and Lindsborg, Kansas, would one day be located.) The Spaniards increasingly became disappointed and discouraged. Although Coronado did note that the land appeared to be abundant with good rivers and rich soil, there was no gold. Coronado's men finally turned on the Turk. They angrily tortured him until he admitted he had made everything up. It was all the Spaniards could stand. A Spanish soldier named Perez "put a rope around Turco's neck . . . and choked him to death."[45]

THE LONG MARCH BACK

With the dream of Quivira's riches now vanished before their eyes, the Spaniards began their trek back to Tiguex in late August 1541. With the help of some Quivira Indian guides, the Spaniards followed another route, one that was nearly 350 miles shorter. After his return to Tiguex, Coronado wintered there, disappointed that he had not discovered the riches found earlier by other conquistadors, such as Pizarro and Cortéz. When spring arrived, he left the lands of New Mexico with his equally discontented army and began the wearisome march back to New Spain and Mexico City. All had failed, it seemed. Several priests remained behind to teach the Indians about Christianity. They would be killed shortly after Coronado and his men left. Many of his soldiers abandoned him on the way back, fearing they would be punished for having failed along with their leader to find riches and for their mistreatment of some of the Indians. Although he left Tiguex with 300 soldiers, Coronado arrived in Mexico City with fewer than 100.

Coronado's "failure" would haunt him for the rest of his life. He had left for the northlands certain of himself and of his success. He had returned to New Spain with nearly nothing to show for his efforts and the money the Crown had spent outfitting his expedition. He was a broken man. He had never fully recovered from the head wound he had received during the

(continues on page 60)

THE UNFORTUNATE PRIESTS
OF THE SOUTHWEST

In 1540, Coronado and his vast army of mounted conquistadors and foot soldiers headed north to discover the riches of the Seven Cities of Cíbola. Although they marched in search of gold, silver, and precious jewels, the Spanish also advanced into the region of present-day New Mexico delivering something many Spaniards considered precious—Christianity. Along with the soldiers, Coronado's expedition included priests, Franciscan fathers who were to provide spiritual help to the Spaniards, but also to preach and teach the Indians about their Holy Faith.

One of the priests was Father Marcos de Niza, who had visited the region previously and had told the stories of the great cities of Cíbola that he had seen with his own eyes. But when the Spaniards reached the lands of the north, they did not find Father Marcos's stories to be true. The padre was disgraced, and Coronado sent him back to Mexico City.

But other priests remained with the Spanish exploration party through the two and a half years that Coronado searched throughout the Southwest and Great Plains. Even when Coronado and his men returned to Mexico City, some of the priests chose to remain to minister to the Indians. Unfortunately, they met with sad fates.

Three friars stayed behind in Tiguex—Fathers Juan de Padilla, Luis de Escalona, and Juan de la Cruz (John of the Cross). Each would meet his death in the remote lands that would one day be part of the United States. Fathers de la Cruz and de Escalona remained in the pueblos of the Tiguex, working closely with the Indians in the Bernalillo-Pecos area. As they taught the Indians about Christianity, the brothers angered the local Indian medicine men who considered themselves the spiritual leaders of their people. Although there is no direct proof, it is believed that both friars were put to death by Indians.

As for Father Juan de Padilla, he decided to return to the Indian tribes in the Quiviran villages in the region of present-day Kansas. The Franciscan father took two young men with him who had been orphaned as boys and raised by the Franciscans. A Portuguese soldier had also volunteered to remain with the Franciscan padre to provide protection. The Spaniards reached Quivira and had some success with the Indians. But they were only in these villages for a few months when trouble arose. The Quivira Indians did not like the Spanish priest to minister to other tribes in the region who were their enemies. Father Juan de Padilla was driven by his faith to teach the gospel to all Indians no matter who they were.

The padre would soon be martyred. Quivira warriors ambushed him one day, shooting several arrows into his body. He was then rolled into a ravine and his corpse covered over with rocks. In the attack, the two young men and the Portuguese soldier managed to escape. They left Quivira and eventually returned to Mexico City, where they told the story of how Father Padilla had died.

After Francisco Vázquez de Coronado left New Mexico in 1542, three Franciscan friars stayed behind in the region the Spanish had visited to minister to the Native Americans. One of these friars was Juan de Padilla (depicted here), who became the first Christian martyr in North America when he was killed by the Quiviras in 1542.

(continued from page 57)

battle at Hawikuh. As a result, his speech was impaired, sometimes making it difficult for him to communicate. Coronado was cast aside, losing his reputation as a grand, noble conquistador, as well as his family fortune. Although he remained in Mexico City for the rest of his life, he died a forgotten man in 1554.

Despite Coronado's failure to discover great riches in the lands that would include modern-day New Mexico, he succeeded in opening up this region of the northlands to Spanish colonization and settlement. Unfortunately, Spanish officials in Mexico City and Madrid were not impressed enough with Coronado's reports of these lands to follow up his explorations with extensive efforts to colonize. To them, once the "Rio Grande Valley produced no . . . wealth for the Spanish crown, the region, considered nothing more than a land of worthless deserts and remote mesas, was almost forgotten."[46] For the next 40 years, the lands that would one day be home to the colonial settlement of Santa Fe were abandoned. It would remain for a new generation of explorers, soldiers, government officials, and priests to return to New Mexico to build a colony. But that day would come.

6

The Spanish Return

By the 1580s and 1590s, after decades of ignoring the lands of modern-day New Mexico, the Spanish began to return to the region. This time they were not pursuing legends that spoke of gold and vast wealth. The first to return were Catholic priests. When Coronado and his men abandoned the region in 1542 and returned to New Spain having failed to discover the gold of the Seven Cities of Cíbola, it was Franciscan priests who remained to teach the gospel to the Indians. Those priests had been martyred, killed for their faith. Now, it would be a new generation of Spanish priests who would lead the march back into the lands that the Spanish Crown had long decided were not worth the blood of its subjects.

NEW EXPLORATIONS

This new generation of Spaniards who entered the Rio Grande Valley, where Santa Fe would one day stand, did not follow Coronado's route. They chose, instead, to take a more direct path. Coronado had swung wide across the Southwest, crossing Arizona into northern New Mexico and beyond. These new arrivals followed the Conchos River—one of the tributaries of the Rio Grande—which flowed to the north out of central Mexico.

Beginning in 1581, a series of four exploratory expeditions followed this new route. The first group consisted of three Franciscan friars led by Father Agustin Rodriguez. This party of holy men was accompanied by 9 soldiers and 16 native Mexican servants. The soldiers marched under the command of Captain Francisco Sánchez Chamuscado. The mission of the fathers was to teach Christianity to the Pueblo Indians. In time, the Spaniards reached the villages that Coronado had marched to, including the pueblo complex at Tiguex. After continuing on to the western edge of the Great Plains, the party turned back west and arrived at Acoma Pueblo along the Zuni River, where Coronado had also visited. Then, at the pueblo at Puaray, the friars remained, sending the soldiers back to Mexico City to report their findings. It was north of Puaray that the settlement of Santa Fe would one day be established.

The next year, another expedition went north, led by Father Bernardino Beltrán. He was accompanied by 19 soldiers and some servants. The soldiers were under the direct command of Antonio de Espejo. By early December 1582, the party reached the banks of the Rio Grande, which they named *Rio del Norte*, the Northern River. Later in the month, they reached the pueblo at Puaray, only to be told that the friars who had arrived the previous year had been killed. Father Beltrán and Espejo did not abandon the Rio Grande region, however. They continued to explore, reaching the Great Plains and seeing their first American bison. They visited several Indian villages and pueblos, including Acoma. They encountered Indians who remembered Coronado from 40 years earlier. They even stumbled upon a traveling chest that had belonged to Coronado, as well as one of his personal books.

In 1582, a group of Spanish explorers led by Father Bernardino Beltrán reached the banks of the Rio Grande, which they named Rio del Norte, or Northern River. Since 1845, the Rio Grande has marked the border between the state of Texas and Mexico.

In time, the father and the soldier decided to split up so they could explore more territory. On his leg of the journey, Espejo came into contact with Indians who told him of valuable silver mines that existed in the region of Acoma Pueblo. Unlike earlier legends of golden cities, Espejo's Indian guides led him to these mines. He later described what he saw: "I found them, and with my own hands, I extracted ore from them, said by those who know to be very rich and contain much silver."[47] Here was another, new incentive for the Spanish to return to the lands of New Mexico. Espejo remained in the region through most of 1583. When he finally returned to Mexico City, his report interested Spanish officials. He explained the lands and the river system more clearly than anyone ever had. He also proposed that the Spanish establish a colony in the Valley of the Rio Grande. He even gave this new Spanish kingdom a name—New Andalusia.

But Spanish officials did not respond immediately by establishing such a northern colony. For one thing, it took years for any idea to make its way through the Spanish bureaucracy. For seven years, proposals for a colony were batted back and forth between Mexico City and Madrid. But, even before a colony was approved, someone decided to establish his own colony without permission. In 1590, a party of 170 Spanish colonists were sent north into New Mexico. They were led by the lieutenant governor of New Leon, Gaspar Castaño de Sosa. The colony was established in present-day northern New Mexico at Santo Domingo (north of present-day Albuquerque). Then, Spanish officials received word of Castaño's illegal colonizing effort. Soldiers were sent to arrest him and his entire mining colony. The lieutenant governor was put on trial and found guilty. He was sent into exile to the Philippines but was killed en route.

Castaño would not be the only Spanish official to try and establish an unauthorized colony in New Mexico. Two Spanish captains, Francisco Leyva de Bonilla and Antonio Gutierrez de Humana, decided to launch their own colony in 1593 without the proper permission. (They had first been sent into the region to put down some Indian uprisings.) When their mission was completed, the two captains decided to march farther north rather than return to Mexico City as ordered. They took along any soldiers who were willing to follow them.

The Leyva-Gutierrez expedition did not go well. Using the lands of the Pueblo Indians as their headquarters, the soldiers marched on to Quivira, perhaps reaching the Platte River

Valley in modern-day Nebraska. Along the way, the two captains turned on one another and Gutierrez killed Leyva. Then, the soldiers were attacked by Indians, and all were killed, except for one, who was later adopted into a local Indian tribe. One of the soldier's servants, a Pueblo Indian, would later tell the story to another Spanish official who later led a march of his own into New Mexico. His colonizing expedition was authorized, and his efforts would one day make him the true founder of New Mexico—Juan de Oñate.

THE FATHER OF NEW MEXICO

Many historians refer to the four expeditions into the modern-day American Southwest that took place before Oñate's as the "Rediscovery of New Mexico." They managed to revive Spanish interest in the region and marked the beginning of the events that ended with Spanish settlement in New Mexico.

When Oñate established his settlement in 1598 in New Mexico, he was launching the period of Spanish colonization of the Southwest. This period continued for more than the next two centuries, only to come to an end in 1821, when Mexico gained its independence from Spain. The seeds for the colony were planted when, in 1595, Don Juan de Oñate, a Creole, offered to use his own money to establish a colony in the north. Oñate was a wealthy nobleman and general who had made a fortune from mining silver in the Mexican province of Zacatecas. With stories of silver mines in New Mexico, Oñate was lured to the north in hopes of finding more riches. By 1598, his dreams had become reality. (His plans had been delayed by Spanish politics and the appointment of a new viceroy of New Spain. Oñate had been friends with the previous viceroy.) Early that year, he set out for New Mexico with 400 soldiers and settlers. The party was accompanied by 10 friars. Oñate had requested the friars to provide "conversion and pacification of the natives."[48] More than 80 squeaky-wheeled wagons were filled with supplies, and herders drove 7,000 head of livestock to supply fresh meat to the group of hopeful colonists. These were the first four-wheeled vehicles to reach today's American Southwest.

By summer, the party had reached the Indian pueblo at Ohke, located on the east bank near where the Chama River flowed into the Rio Grande. This became the colony's headquarters, which they named San Juan Bautista (the site was later renamed San Gabriel). The Indians living nearby were the Tewa tribe. As the colonists began building homes, the priests fanned out in search of natives to teach and convert. Colonists soon discovered an abandoned Indian silver mine, which they began working. The Spanish colonists also built one of the first churches in what would later become the United States. (It was actually the second, for the first had already been erected in St. Augustine in Florida.)

The first winter at San Juan was difficult. Despite all the supplies they had taken, the colonists suffered food shortages. There were also problems with the Zunis. A violent encounter took place at Acoma Pueblo, which Coronado had visited 60 years earlier. It began when a nephew of Oñate's, Juan de Zaldívar, led a party of 30 soldiers to the pueblo. Acoma was a spectacular pueblo complex set upon a 367-foot-high mesa with a commanding view of the New Mexico plains. It is still an Indian pueblo today, and is believed to be the oldest continually inhabited town in the United States. Zaldivar and half his men decided to climb the mesa and meet with the Indians there and ask them for fresh supplies. The Indians appeared friendly, at first, but soon turned on the Spaniards, killing them one by one. Only five survived. They fought their way through a host of Indian warriors until they were cornered on a ledge of the mesa. With no choice, the surviving Spaniards jumped off the mesa.

Acoma Pueblo, pictured here in 1904, sits atop a 367-foot sandstone mesa, 60 miles west of present-day Albuquerque, New Mexico. In 1598, Acoma was the site of a battle between its Zuni residents and the Spanish, which resulted in the town being abandoned for nearly 100 years.

Although it is not known where they jumped from, the shortest jump would have been 160 feet! One of the soldiers was killed in the fall, but the other four miraculously survived. As they told their story later, they landed in "some sand which the wind had blown up against the foot of the mesa."[49] These four soon rejoined the remainder of their force that Zaldívar had left at the base of the mesa. High above in the city of Acoma, 13 Spanish soldiers lay dead, including Zaldívar.

THE BATTLE FOR "SKY CITY"

The "massacre" of Spanish soldiers brought about another march to Acoma. Oñate dispatched another of his nephews, Juan's brother Vicente de Zaldívar, to the mesa for revenge. Zaldívar marched 70 men to Acoma—the "Sky City"—and prepared to launch an attack. When he arrived, the Zunis gathered on the edge of their mesa and shouted insults down to the Spaniards. Some began "dancing stark naked," which the Spaniards interpreted as an insult.[50] With most of his men attacking from one direction, Zaldívar sent a smaller group of soldiers up the cliff walls with a small cannon. They managed to reach the top of the mesa without being seen, completely surprising the Zunis. They were then joined by Zaldívar's main force. A three-day battle unfolded, resulting in the deaths of most of the Zuni warriors. Approximately 600 of the 3,000 natives who lived at Acoma chose to commit suicide by leaping off the mesa rather than be taken prisoner by the Spanish. However, about 75 men, women, and children were taken as prisoners, and the Spaniards then set the city on fire. (Some of the Zunis who escaped that day returned to Acoma and built a new village at the foot of the summit, leaving their burned-out city empty. It was not until 1680 that another generation of Zunis returned to the top of the mesa and rebuilt Sky City.)

The captives were taken by Zaldívar to San Juan, where they were severely punished. Of the men, everyone under the age of 25 was given a term of 20 years' service to the Spanish. All men over that age were punished by having a foot cut off. As for the women and children, they were forced into virtual slavery. Because of the severe treatment given to the Zunis, the Oñate colony had no further significant trouble with the natives of the region.

A TROUBLED COLONY

But, even without serious Indian challenges, the colony that Oñate established in the deserts of New Mexico faced other problems. One of them was Oñate himself. While many of his colonists (several had migrated north with their entire

A FRANCISCAN RETURNS TO SKY CITY

Long after the residents of Acoma had been defeated by Zaldívar and his men in the late 1590s, the Indians who lived at the mesa remained hostile toward the Spaniards. Nevertheless, a brave Spanish Franciscan, Father Juan Ramirez, decided to go to Acoma to establish a mission among these Indians. As the story goes, Father Ramirez walked to the pueblo alone across the desert. When he reached Acoma, the Zunis angrily shouted down that he should leave. The Franciscan padre, however, began to climb the cliff walls, even as the Zunis fired arrows at him. Some of them "pierced the cloth of his grey habit."*

Then, suddenly, a small Indian girl, who was watching the unfolding scene from the mesa's ledge, lost her balance and fell. She toppled out of sight of the Zunis above, but landed on a ledge just a few yards from Father Ramirez. He was able to rescue her and carry her in his arms up to the top of the mesa. Believing the Franciscan father had performed a miracle and saved one of their own, the Zunis at Acoma befriended Father Ramirez and allowed him to remain in their desert town.

Father Ramirez lived at Acoma for the next 20 years. He converted the Zunis and taught them to read and write. He even had them build a church dedicated to Saint Stephen the King—*San Esteban del Rey*. The church was later damaged during the Pueblo Revolt in 1680. (Father Ramirez was killed during that uprising.) That church remains today and is one of the best examples of New Mexican mission architecture. (The church is only used today during the Acoma fiesta celebrations.) Tourists who visit Acoma Pueblo are still reminded of Father Ramirez. The stone stairway-trail that is used to reach the pueblo town is called *El Camino del Padre*, the Path of the Father.

* Albert J. Nevins, *Our American Catholic Heritage* (Huntington, Ind.: Our Sunday Visitor, Inc., 1972), 62.

families) worked hard and tried to farm the land, Oñate seemed more interested in being an explorer than a colonizer. He was a latter-day Coronado, "still eager to find gold and glory."[51] He went out on explorations, leaving his colonists to fend for themselves. By 1601, there were serious accusations against Oñate for his mismanagement of the colony. (Others wrote to the viceroy describing Oñate as a good administrator and governor.) By 1605, the Council of the Indies, which monitored the Spanish colonies in the Americas, recommended that Oñate be replaced and that he be investigated. In 1607, Oñate resigned.

With Oñate removed from his position, authorities in New Spain were forced to decide whether or not the new colony in New Mexico should continue or be abandoned. In 1608, before a decision could be made, authorities gave an audience to a Franciscan friar, Lazaro Ximenez, who had worked among the Indians in the region. He claimed that 7,000 Indians had been converted to Christianity. (Whether the number is accurate or not is not clear.)

With that number of conversions claimed, the Spanish government did not want to abandon the New Mexican colony. The viceroy of New Spain, Luis de Velasco, who had earlier supported abandoning New Mexico, suddenly wrote to the king in Madrid, Philip III: "We could not abandon the land without great offense to God and great risk of losing what has been gained."[52] The decision was made to turn New Mexico into a royal colony with a new governor. (Neither Oñate or his son Cristobal would be given any claim to the colony.) Authorities also decided to designate New Mexico "a missionary field with friars maintained at royal expense."[53]

The future of New Mexico would be forever changed. With religion, not wealth, as the incentive for colonization, the Spanish decided to focus their efforts on colonizing this land in the bleak deserts of the northlands. Also, the colony was being taken over by the Crown and was no longer the responsibility of private owners, such as Oñate. As for Oñate, he was replaced by another governor, Don Pedro de Peralta.

7

The Founding of Santa Fe

Governor Juan de Oñate resigned as the leader of his own personal colony in 1607. Even then, the viceroy of New Spain ordered him to remain in New Mexico and operate the colony until his replacement was selected. Once he was allowed to return to Mexico City, Oñate had to account for the mismanagement of his colony. Back in New Spain, Oñate went on trial, charged with poor leadership, mistreatment of the colonists, soldiers, and Indians, and disobedience to the viceroy. Spanish officials found him guilty of several of the charges by 1614. The former colonizer of New Mexico was fined 6,000 ducats, not a small sum, and banished from New Mexico for the rest of his life. He was also banned from Mexico City for four years. Although he appealed the government's decisions, he never succeeded in getting a pardon from the Spanish monarch. By 1625, he died, having never regained his earlier status.

A NEW GOVERNOR ARRIVES

The new governor was not selected until 1609. He was another Spanish aristocrat, Don Pedro de Peralta. Not only was he appointed governor, he was to serve the New Mexico colony as captain-general. While the colony had been a drain on Governor Oñate's personal fortune, Peralta was to receive 2,000 pesos annually. He arrived in New Mexico in the fall of 1609 and set out immediately to reorganize the colony. In an effort to make the colony more secure, he first moved the main settlement, San Gabriel, away from the local Indian pueblos to a new site.

His new colony would center around the settlement he would call La Villa Real de la Santa Fe de San Francisco (The Royal City of the Holy Faith of St. Francis). It was a well-intended name, but too long for people to say. Peralta decided to shorten it to Santa Fe. With the establishment of this new capital, Santa Fe, New Mexico, would one day be known as the oldest capital in what would become the United States. (It was not the oldest city, of course. There was the Indian town at Acoma, and the Spanish had earlier established St. Augustine in Florida.) The complete transfer of the Spanish royal colony to its new capital took place in 1610.

The new settlement site was well chosen. Peralta selected "a pleasant location on the fertile banks of a tributary to the upper Rio Grande, about 75 miles above Tiguex."[54] The new governor even paced off the site, marking the ground that would become Santa Fe's central common, the *plaza de armas*, or parade ground. He then ordered, using Indian labor, the construction of the *casas reales*—the royal house of government that would house the governor's official residence. This "palace of the governor" also included his official "offices," as well as the headquarters for the local military garrison. These first buildings constructed at Santa Fe were not elaborate, just simple low-roofed adobe structures.

The move from San Gabriel to Santa Fe was a good decision by Peralta. It eliminated some of the Indian-Spanish conflicts. This new capital site was located farther south of

The Old Palace of the Governors was originally constructed in 1609–1610 to serve as the governor of Nuevo México's official residence. The building, which is today the home of a state history museum, is thought to be the oldest continually occupied public structure in the United States.

the pueblo villages. But the Spanish colonial capital did not thrive during the years that followed. One aspect of Spanish colonialism that did work fairly well was the efforts made by the Catholic Church through its Franciscan priests. Other holy men had entered New Mexico in earlier generations and had limited success at best. Several of these first priests had been killed by Indians who did not understand their ways or the new faith they tried to convince the New Mexico natives they should embrace as their own. The general mission of these Franciscan fathers was to convert the Indians and convince them to accept Spanish rule. They also worked hard to train the Indians to become primarily farmers. To do so meant these Indians were expected to give up their ways of warfare and the raiding they sometimes carried out against their enemy tribes, as well as the Spanish themselves. In exchange, the Spanish promised protection to the Indians who converted. Such protection took the form of the local *presidio*, or fortress, that housed the soldiers in the region.

For many years, the Franciscan priests struggled to convert as many of the estimated 40,000 Indians who lived along the upper reaches of the Rio Grande Valley in and around Santa Fe as they could, as well as those living along the Little Colorado and Upper Zuni rivers located to the west. Records indicate that between 1601 and 1607, the Franciscans baptized perhaps as many as 600 Indians; perhaps as few as 60. Each priest who was sent to a particular Indian group had to learn its language. There were four basic language groups spoken in the region during the early 1600s, as well as dozens of less-spoken dialects. Through their diligent efforts, the Franciscan padres successfully converted thousands of Indians in New Mexico.

The Franciscans established their own headquarters at Santo Domingo, approximately 30 miles south and west of Santa Fe. The missionary priests not only taught the gospel but European skills and crafts, such as carpentry, stone working, blacksmithing, masonry, and other arts. The Indians became skilled in the use of European tools, and with their new talents, helped construct churches throughout the the Southwest.

By 1611, the colony established by Peralta was taking root. Everything seemed to be improving and the colony was becoming more stable:

> By the time the cottonwoods along the rivers began to turn green in the spring of 1611, Peralta could begin to appreciate some of the changes the Spanish had brought to an Indian world. From his newly built palace-fortress on the plaza, the Governor could watch horses, cattle, goats and sheep grazing on hillsides where only the Indian dog and the turkey had been seen before. New crops sprouted in the irrigated fields—oats, barley, wheat, onions, peas, melons and varieties of beans hitherto unknown to the Indians. Young fruit trees were blossoming.[55]

Spanish agriculture and animal husbandry were taking their places throughout the lands surrounding Santa Fe.

GROWTH OF A COLONIAL OUTPOST

These were critical years for the colony based at Santa Fe. The colonists were stuck in a remote region more than 1,000 miles from the capital of New Spain, Mexico City. It was important that a connection between the two be maintained, especially the trade route. Every three years, beginning in 1609, royal caravans reached Santa Fe from Mexico City. The heavy, wooden supply carts were filled with much-needed supplies and provisions for the colony. Items needed for the local mission churches, including artwork, candleholders, altarpieces, and other ecclesiastical items were delivered, as well as other manufactured goods that could not then be produced on the frontier of New Mexico. The colonists then reloaded the carts with local trade goods, such as animal hides, leather, Indian-produced textiles, salt, and other commodities. This exchange—manufactured goods for raw materials and natural goods—provided a trade base for Santa Fe that went far beyond bartering with local Indians. The arrival of the royal caravan from one capital to another was the "one regularly scheduled contact the Upper Rio Grande colony had with Mexico City and mainstream Spanish civilization."[56] In time, a road between the two developed—*El Camino Real*, or the Royal Road. It was a long, snaky route that passed across difficult terrain through northern Mexico and southern New Mexico. It was such a difficult road to travel, one lined with deserts baked with a hot sun, that the Spaniards unofficially named it *La Jornado del Muerto*, the Journey of the Dead.

Governor Peralta had established the settlement site that he would name Santa Fe in the spring of 1610, a location that placed the colonial capital of New Mexico near where the Chama River and the Rio Grande came together. It was also at the southern end of the Sangre de Cristo (translated "the blood of Christ") Mountains. The plan for the community was to begin with the laying out of "six vecindades [districts] for the villa and a square block for government buildings [casas reales, later known as the Palace of the Governors] and other public works."[57] Peralta not only laid out the building scheme, he also established the system of government of Santa Fe. It would include four *regidores*, or councilmen. Two of them were to serve as *alcaldes ordinarios*, or judges. They were responsible for hearing court cases, both civil and criminal, that took place around Santa Fe. One of these two judges was to serve as *justicia mayor*, the high judge, of the community.

Peralta gave these alcaldes and regidores much power and authority in Santa Fe. It was in their hands to assign "to each resident two lots for house and garden, two contiguous fields for vegetable gardens, two others for vineyards and olive groves, and in addition four caballerias [approximately 133 acres] of land; and for irrigation, the necessary water."[58] But these land grants were not given without some expectations. The colonists were to agree to live on and improve their lands for 10 years. Anyone leaving their lands in the hands of others for as long as four months had to get permission from the *cabildo*, or town council, or lose his property.

During its first two years of settlement, between 1610 and 1612, Santa Fe grew. Additional government buildings were constructed, including a jail, a chapel, and an arsenal. These

THE PALACE OF THE GOVERNORS

Today, tourists who visit Santa Fe are captivated by the city's unique Southwestern culture, its arts, and its architecture. The city is home to a multiethnic culture, a blending of Native American, Hispanic, and Anglo-American history, art, and daily life. At every turn, visitors see a mix of modern and traditional buildings. Even many of those structures built today have the appearance and style of the adobe architecture that has dominated the urban landscapes of New Mexico for centuries. But a highlight for nearly every tourist who visits the city today is a building that still serves as the state's history museum and is among the oldest built by the Spanish—the Palace of the Governors.

It is probably the oldest public building, not just in New Mexico, but in the United States. Governor Peralta himself was responsible for laying out the grounds where the palace was constructed, beginning in 1610. Since its construction, this most important of New Mexico's public buildings has remained one of the most important places in the nearly four-hundred-year history of Santa Fe. It has gone by various names. When first constructed, it was the *casas reales*, the royal houses. The building complex was also known then as the *palacio real*, the royal palace. By the early twentieth century, it was known as either the *adobe palace* or *el palacio*.

Archaeologists have revealed that the oldest parts of the palace were constructed by placing small logs standing vertically in rows in a trench, then caulked between with mud. Archaeologists do not all agree about the dimensions of the early Palace of the Governors. Most believe that the palace grounds included a square compound that was situated north of the back walls of today's Palace of the Governors. Over the centuries, the palace grounds and the buildings themselves changed. Although the enclosed patio around the palace was likely 350 feet or so on each side of the public building's grounds, the patio is only about one-quarter that size today. Many buildings were surrounded by a defensive wall to provide protection for the government compound, which included the Palace of the Governors. Throughout the capital, businesses opened, and the town's population included "farmers, artisans, traders, missionaries, and other frontiersmen and their Indian servants."[59] Santa Fe became such an important colonial outpost that all the roads in the region, especially the

of the palace's specific buildings either do not exist today or have been dramatically changed.

One significant change to the Palace of the Governors took place during the Pueblo Revolt of 1680. Once the Spanish had left the city, the Pueblo Indians tore down much of the building they believed had a Spanish appearance. They then remodeled the *casas reales* along the lines of one of their pueblo buildings. Archaeologists believe that, during the Indian occupation, many of the palace's rooms were carved into smaller rooms typically found in a pueblo. Even the doors and windows were covered over with adobe and the Indians cut holes in the roof, entering the structure with ladders, just a they did in their pueblos.

So many changes were made to the palace during the Pueblo Revolt that it is impossible to know exactly what the original palace looked like. Although the exact design of the earlier models of the Palace of the Governors remain unknown, one thing is certain: It looked much different during the early 1600s than it does today. Even its most distinctive feature—the long covered "porch" that faces out onto Santa Fe's plaza—has undergone many changes through the years. By the end of the nineteenth century, that front portico had been updated with a more modern Victorian look.

However, by the early years of the twentieth century, yet another change was made to the front portico. During some repairs prior to 1910, an original front column was uncovered in an adobe wall. The School of American Archaeology, which would later become the School of American Research, then set out to restore the front portico for the last time. Their work changed the portico back to what might have been the original style of the Palace of the Governors. Today's tourists, then, have an opportunity to see the four-centuries-old palace much as it looked during its early years.

The Chapel of San Miguel was built between 1610 and 1626 but was damaged during the Pueblo Revolt of 1680 and rebuilt in 1710. Although it is not the oldest church in the United States, its adobe walls have largely remained intact for nearly 500 years.

Camino Real de Tierra Adentro, the Royal Road of the Interior, ran through it.

Small neighborhoods were formed in early Santa Fe. One was a section of the town called the *Barrio de Analco*. This was a Mexican-Indian community established on the other side of the Rio Grande. (*Analco* means "on the other side.") The Indians living here farmed fields that were connected to the chapel of San Miguel. As Peralta established his government and its systems in Santa Fe, another local "leader," Father Alonso de Peinado, was establishing his own. (The two men had arrived in Santa Fe together having traveled from Mexico City on the same wagon caravan in 1608.) Friar Peinado, then in his late 50s, was the Franciscan brother in charge of all the missions in New Mexico. He oversaw the construction of a church for Santa Fe, so the local people would have a place to worship. (The earlier church was a simple building fashioned out of mud mortar.) In 1610, Father Peinado established his church "headquarters" at Santo Domingo Pueblo, which was located south of Santa Fe. It was important that the church have its own "ecclesiastical" capital separate from the "civil government" capital at Santa Fe. Between 1610 and 1611, each of these "capitals" of New Mexico was in its early stages, and Governor Peralta and Father Peinado remained on friendly terms. Each was carving his place in the early colonial history of the region.

8

The Peralta-
Ordoñez Affair

The efforts of Governor Pedro de Peralta to establish an important colonial city in New Mexico would bear fruit. During the years 1610 to 1615, the new community of Santa Fe took root. But this process was not without problems. Between those two dates, a struggle for power in Santa Fe would take place. The struggle would involve two strong opponents—Governor Peralta, the founder of Santa Fe, and Father Isidro Ordoñez. The conflict was not only between two men but between the power of the state and the power of the Church.

THE ARRIVAL OF FATHER ORDOÑEZ

Near the end of the summer of 1612, Friar Isidro Ordoñez, along with a dozen fellow missionaries, arrived at the mission center at Santo Domingo. The friar soon announced that he had been sent with papers authorizing him to replace Father Peinado. Although Father Peinado was skeptical of Father Ordoñez's papers, the padre agreed to step down. Soon, Father Ordoñez was in Santa Fe, informing Peralta that the padre was there to replace the governor as the highest official in New Mexico.

Ordoñez's papers also seemed to authorize any of Peralta's colonists, including his soldiers, to leave the colony if they wanted to. The governor soon became suspicious of the padre's papers, which the Franciscan claimed had been signed by the viceroy of New Spain himself.

Father Ordoñez had been in New Mexico before. He had served in the colony under Juan de Oñate and was not liked by the majority of Franciscans in the region. One of those padres, Friar Francisco Perez Huerta, who was an official notary, which gave him regular access to official documents, looked at Ordoñez's papers to verify their authenticity. Huerta did not believe them to be legitimate. But Huerta did not examine the papers until four years after Friar Ordoñez arrived at the Palace of the Governors to claim he was the high authority of New Mexico. Governor Peralta had known Ordoñez before and did not like the friar's insistence that he take control of the colony. The governor did not even like Ordoñez replacing Peinado. When he first received word of Peinado's replacement, Peralta exclaimed: "Would to God the devil were coming instead of that friar!"[60]

Things did not go well between the governor and the insistent friar. However, Peralta continued to serve as governor, and the two men were able to avoid a direct confrontation until the spring of 1613. That May, Friar Ordoñez made a move to interfere with one of the governor's official privileges. Each year, the governor's office was to collect a "contribution" of corn and blankets from the local pueblos. When the tribute collectors made their way to Taos Pueblo, north of Santa Fe, Father Ordoñez ordered them to return to the town for the Feast of the Pentecost, a holy celebration. They returned to Santa Fe empty-handed, only to be ordered by one of the governor's military officers to return to their duties at Taos Pueblo.

Later that month, the governor and the church father crossed paths in the town plaza and began to argue about the

Taos Pueblo, pictured here in 1915, has been inhabited for more than 1,000 years. During the time of Spanish control, tribute collectors were often sent to pueblos such as Taos to collect payment from the local Indian tribes.

matter. The governor claimed he had the authority to order his collectors to carry out their necessary duties. The friar claimed he had the authority to counter the governor's orders, because they violated a holy day on the church calendar. After showing the governor yet another official paper, this one recognizing Ordoñez as the head of the Inquisition for New Mexico, the friar ordered Peralta to recall his agents who were on their way to Taos. (The Inquisition was an official Catholic body whose intent was to protect the Church by seeking out heresy and those who violated church law.) If the governor would not do as Ordoñez said, the friar threatened to excommunicate Peralta, which would mean the governor would not be allowed to partake in Mass or any other church function. An angry Governor Peralta refused to do as the Franciscan padre instructed him. Ordoñez soon followed up on his threat, and nailed the governor's excommunication to the door of the Santa Fe church.

An immediate storm of controversy spilled out into the public arena. Townspeople in Santa Fe were shocked at the excommunication and begged their governor to repent. He refused. One friar offered to secretly forgive the governor of his sin against the church to avoid a public confession on the part of Peralta. Again, the governor refused. The confrontation came to a head. Finally, the two strong-willed men agreed to put their differences aside and Ordoñez gave the governor absolution, or official forgiveness.

But the priest and governor did not stay on friendly terms for long. Father Ordoñez remained relentless in his harassment of the governor, finding fault with him at every turn. He even went so far as to plot against the governor with another Franciscan to remove Peralta from power. The two holy men planned a special Mass for the captains of the Spanish soldiers in Santa Fe, as well as the town officials, who would include Governor Peralta. When the special Sunday arrived, a servant of Peralta's arrived with the governor's special chair and placed it on its designated platform in the church. Before a packed congregation of the faithful, Friar Ordoñez's coconspirator, Friar Tirado, took the chair and threw it out of the church sanctuary. Finding his chair lying in the dirt outside the church when he arrived, Governor Peralta ordered it put back into place in the church, but at the back of the church, not at the front.

Soon, the special Mass began. Friar Ordoñez took his place at the pulpit in the church and started a sermon that was highly critical of Governor Peralta. He made false claims against the leader of the Santa Fe colony. He told the congregation that he, the friar, was the greater power. "Do not be deceived," said the Franciscan leader. "Let no one persuade himself with vain words that I do not have the same power and authority that the Pope in Rome has, or that if his Holiness were here in New Mexico he could do more than I."[61] Friar Ordoñez preached that only he could "arrest, cast in irons, and punish as seems fitting to me any person without exception who is not obedient to the commandments of the church and mine."[62] As an angry Governor Peralta listened from the back of the church, Father Ordoñez taunted him, as he spoke to the congregation: "What I have told you I say for the benefit of a certain person who is listening to me who perhaps raises his eyebrows."[63]

After the completion of the special Mass, the entire town of Santa Fe was talking about what Father Ordoñez had said and how he had treated the governor. It did not take long before the two powerful men found another reason to face off with one another. Just days following the special Mass, Father Ordoñez ordered the governor arrested by his fellow Franciscans over an order Peralta had given to one of his soldiers. The soldier was also the one responsible for collecting the church tithes (small taxes or levies) in the region and reporting to Father Ordoñez. Caught between his duties to the governor and the friar, the soldier was ordered by Peralta to resign his position as tithe collector and serve Peralta. Friar Ordoñez felt the order was "an offense against the church."[64] Without a doubt, the governor and the friar were on a collision course.

THE GOVERNOR AND THE FRIAR SQUARE OFF

By July 9, Peralta, feeling something had to be done about Friar Ordoñez's belief that he was the true leader of the colony, rallied the colonists in and around Santa Fe on his behalf. The governor called as many as would come to the Palace of the Governors, armed and ready for action. Several came to his aid. Gathering his supporters in his private quarters, Peralta informed the New Mexicans that the friar was about to arrest him. But they would strike the first blow, said the governor. They would rise up and turn out the friar from Santa Fe. It was to be a showdown between the secular leader of the colony and the local head of the Church. Peralta armed himself and gathered up a force of additional armed men. When they approached the friar, and Peralta ordered him to leave Santa Fe, violence broke out. Before it was all over, Peralta had accidentally shot another Franciscan (see sidebar on pages 88–89).

In the days that followed, the Franciscans in the region gathered at Santo Domingo to discuss what should happen next. After all, one of their own brothers had been shot. Soon, Father Ordoñez returned to Santa Fe, calling for the arrest of Governor Peralta for attempted murder. But no one was willing to support the padre. They did not want to get involved any further in the clashes between the governor and the friar.

Father Ordoñez then set a trap for Governor Peralta. He knew that the governor would either send word to Mexico City, informing officials of his local clashes with the friar, or he would try to get to the capital of New Spain himself. On August 12, Peralta was caught at Isleta Pueblo, where he was tracked down by Father Ordoñez and some Indians and settlers who had joined him against the governor.

Over the next eight months, the humiliated Governor Peralta was held prisoner in a jail at the Sandia Pueblo, wearing shackles. In his place, Father Ordoñez ruled over Santa Fe with a heavy hand. He threatened the people of the town and region with his power. Even some of his fellow Franciscans were appalled at his behavior. As one friar wrote: "Excommunications were rained down . . . and because of the terrors that worked abroad the people were not only scandalized but afraid . . . existence in [Santa Fe] was a hell."[65]

One night, however, Peralta managed to escape and fled across the open country, skirting around Santo Domingo. Three days later, in late March 1614, he reached Santa Fe, where he hid in the house of a friend. Still wearing his shackles, the governor was badly worn from his escape, having not eaten for days. He had spent two nights outdoors in the cold and snow, which nearly killed him. In the meantime, Father Ordoñez had

A FACE-OFF AND A NEAR DEATH

After months of conflict, Governor Peralta and Father Ordoñez had one of their most serious showdowns in early July 1613. Peralta gathered a force of armed supporters and went to the *convento* (convent) in Santa Fe to confront the hated padre.

As the governor and his followers approached the convento next to the church in the town, the local priests watched them and ran to tell Father Ordoñez. At that same moment, a group of women, mostly the wives of those following Peralta, entered the church for the regular morning Mass. When Father Ordoñez entered the sanctuary, he found many of the women crying. They were afraid that the powerful friar would excommunicate their husbands.

Outside, Peralta and his men approached the *porteria*, the gate of the convent. The governor was ready for anything, wearing a "coat of chain mail, armed with a sword in his belt, and carrying a pistolet [a small pistol] in his hand."* Peralta and his sympathizers waited outside the church until Father Ordoñez completed the Mass. Knowing the governor was outside in the convento yard, the friar took up a wooden cane and went to meet face-to-face with Peralta. Once the two men encountered each other, the governor gave orders to the padre to leave Santa Fe and return to his headquarters at the pueblo at Santo Domingo. Ordoñez refused, and the two men began throwing insults and curses at one another. Brandishing his pistol, the governor ordered his men to enter the convento buildings to look for any weapons. An angry Father Ordoñez shouted to them all that he would excommunicate every man standing before him. The governor responded loudly that he would order the arrest of Father Ordoñez.

learned of the governor's escape and soon reached the New Mexico capital, ordering his supporters to search for Peralta. The governor was soon discovered and taken to Santo Domingo, "on a horse, and covered with a hide."[66] When he arrived at Father Ordoñez's headquarters, the padre put Peralta on public display and humiliated him, telling all those gathered that the governor was not above the law and that justice would soon be served. Peralta was held as a prisoner over the next year in a small cell at Zia Pueblo.

Then, a fight broke out between the two men and everything became chaotic:

> Peralta grabbed Ordoñez's cape, and the friar slapped away his hand. Other priests moved in to defend their prelate. Friar Tirado took a sword from one of the soldiers and thrust it at Peralta, ripping his cape. While Ordoñez tried to hit the governor with his cane, Peralta raised his pistolet, but someone grabbed him by the wrist and the gun went off. . . . The pungent smoke which filled the room brought everyone to a standstill. Friar Pedraza fell to the floor; he had been shot. Luckily, he had only been superficially wounded, but the shocking sight of a priest lying in pain on the floor cast a different character on the governor's actions. Slowly, Peralta's followers began to drift out of the room and away from him.[**]

The confrontation between the governor and the friar had ended as abruptly as it had begun. Before the day was over, Father Ordoñez had nailed up notices of the governor's excommunication, as well as that of some of his followers.

* David Grant Noble, *Santa Fe: History of an Ancient City* (Santa Fe, N.M.: School of American Research Press, 1989), 35.
** Ibid.

A NEW GOVERNOR FOR SANTA FE

By 1615, the viceroy appointed a new governor for New Mexico. He was Bernardino de Ceballos, who had earlier in his career served as an admiral in the Spanish Armada. Word of his approach to Santo Domingo sent Father Ordoñez out to greet him. The encounter did not go well for the ambitious friar. Ceballos was not impressed with Ordoñez and did not take long to state his intentions. He told the friar: "Are you the same *padre missionero* who represents himself as most powerful and exacting, whom I have met before?"[67] The new governor informed the friar that he would soon release Peralta and "honor him . . . as a governor deserves."[68]

After his arrival in Santa Fe, the new governor ordered the release of Peralta, although a month lapsed before the former governor was actually set free. But Peralta's problems were not completely over. Governor Ceballos soon summoned a *residencia*, an official investigation into the Peralta governship. Throughout the weeks of testimony and fact-finding, Father Ordoñez managed to intimidate many of Peralta's supporters from testifying on his behalf. Those who did speak at the residencia played down the clash between Peralta and Ordoñez. Nevertheless, Ceballos was not pleased with Ordoñez and his attempt to seize power in Santa Fe. The new governor told the friar that he did not have authority to represent the Inquisition and that Father Ordoñez had never had the power to arrest a governor of the province of New Mexico.

By August, the residencia was completed. Throughout the summer of trying to get to the truth of what had taken place in Santa Fe during the previous two years, the new governor had turned against Peralta. It is unclear why. Peralta was allowed to leave Santa Fe, but much of his property was confiscated. The humiliated governor then set out for Mexico City, where he hoped to explain himself and his earlier actions. He managed to smuggle papers out of Santa Fe, documents that would help him present his case to authorities far to the south. By 1615, an official Mexican Inquisition was held, and Peralta was allowed to present his documents and speak out on his own behalf. By October 1617, the case was decided. Peralta was found innocent of any charges that had been leveled against him. As for Father Ordoñez, he was ordered to Mexico City, where he was seriously chastised for taking too much power upon himself without the proper authority.

9

Santa Fe Survives

The clash between Governor Pedro Peralta and Father Isidro Ordoñez was a setback for the fledgling colony centered in Santa Fe. But in the years that followed, the colony continued to grow and even flourish as an outpost in the northlands of the Spanish New World Empire.

SUCCESS FOR THE FRANCISCANS

Despite the harm done by Father Ordoñez, the Franciscans continued their efforts in the region, working with the thousands of Indians in New Mexico. In 1621, the Franciscans reported that they had converted more than 60,000 Indians throughout the New Mexico colony. (This figure may have been an overestimate, because another Franciscan report, written in 1680, placed the number of Indian converts at fewer than 30,000.) In the year 1630, an ecclesiastical report was sent to the Spanish monarch informing His Majesty that "50 friars were at work in 90 villages, and that each village had its own church." By that same year, just a generation after the founding of Santa Fe, the town was no longer a tiny outpost; rather, it had become the most important Spanish town within hundreds of miles. More than 1,000 Spaniards called Santa Fe home. An additional 1,000 Spanish residents lived on ranches and farms dotting the deserts of the region. But the region was still considered unsafe. Of the 1,000 residents of the New Mexican capital, one in four was a soldier.

Throughout the remainder of the seventeenth century, the New Mexico colony based in Santa Fe continued to develop, take root, and ultimately thrive. It was never a colony without problems, however. There would be other clashes between the Franciscans and various governmental leaders. Many of the colonists in New Mexico did not prosper and lived in relative poverty. These colonists were sometimes envious of the wealth centered on the Catholic-administered mission lands, where the Pueblo Indian populations were typically exploited. The Indians worked at the missions as part of their tribute to the Spanish Crown. Sometimes governors claimed jurisdiction over these church properties, their Indians, and the friars themselves. This caused friction between the secular rulers of New Mexico and the churchmen who were there in the name of the pope.

The exploitation of the Indians was not always done by the Franciscans or other church fathers. Governors were sometimes accused of mistreating the native populations, as well. Some of these governors became so notorious for collecting personal wealth at the expense of the local Indians that they were investigated, found guilty, and replaced by other governors. Some were jailed and even excommunicated by the Catholic Church. One such governor was Diego de Peñalosa, who administered the colony from 1661 to 1664. He was eventually brought to trial by the Church and found guilty of heresy. He was fined, banned from holding any other public office in New Mexico, and ordered to "march barefoot through the streets of Mexico City while carrying a green candle of penitence."[69]

During their attempt to convert Native Americans to Christianity, Franciscan priests often mistreated and exploited them. As a result of this mistreatment, the Pueblo Indians rose up in a massive revolt in 1680 that resulted in 400 Spanish deaths, including 23 priests.

THE PUEBLO REVOLT OF 1680

Clashes between the Church and the secular leaders continued through the remainder of the seventeenth century. But one conflict led to a violent confrontation late in the century that nearly led the Spanish to abandon New Mexico altogether. Because of constant exploitation and mistreatment by the Franciscans and the multiple tributes they were forced to pay to Spanish officials, the Pueblo Indians rose up in revolt in 1680. It was a highly organized and well-led uprising that resulted in gangs of Indian warriors systematically raiding many New Mexican villages, killing Spanish men, women, and children. The Indians also raided mission settlements and they were especially brutal in their treatment of the friars, whom they hated. The day of the revolt, August 13, would be a day that nearly destroyed the future of Santa Fe and the long-standing Spanish effort to successfully colonize New Mexico:

> All through the day reports flooded in [to Santa Fe]. Pecos, Taos, Santa Cruz, San Marcos, San Cristobal, Santo Domingo, Santa Clara, Picuris—all the pueblos in the area had risen, all the churches were being burned, all the priests killed. As far away as Acoma and the Zuni and Hopi villages to the west there was death and destruction. By the night of the 13th, all Spaniards in the Santa Fe area had swarmed into the town. Survivors from the devastated areas to the north and west ran gauntlets of raiding parties to seek safety in Santa Fe.[70]

Over the following week, the capital of Santa Fe was a battleground. Soon after the uprising had begun, Indians descended on the New Mexican capital and virtually surrounded it. Within days, 2,500 Native American warriors were in the fields around Santa Fe, threatening to burn it down. (There were only 150 Spanish soldiers in the local garrison to protect the community.) By August 16, the Indians had gained control of the entire capital except for the plaza grounds. They set fire to the buildings until "the whole town became a torch."[71] The Pueblos cut off the town's water supply by blocking the ditch that delivered water, making firefighting almost impossible. On the following day, Indian besiegers tormented and mocked the beleaguered Spaniards in Santa Fe by chanting the Catholic liturgy in Latin. They were words the Indians had come to despise.

The town held out until August 21. The local leaders then announced they would leave Santa Fe. As the families gathered themselves for the evacuation and the march to the south, they followed along behind "the old yellow silk banner that Spanish soldiers had carried into New Mexico the century before."[72] Before the Pueblo Indian Revolt of 1680, the Spanish population living in Santa Fe and along the Upper Rio Grande was approximately 2,800 people. The uprising resulted in the deaths of 400 Spaniards—one out of seven. Another 400 were missing and

SANTA FE IN 1790

Nearly 200 years after its founding, the New Mexico capital of Santa Fe had become a well-established community. While Spanish officials often kept exact records and papers on many aspects of the colonial experience, the 1790 census is one of the most complete records of the colonial period. It tells modern historians just how much Santa Fe had grown and changed over the years from its founding in the early seventeenth century.

According to the census, Santa Fe was home to 2,542 residents, representing 564 families. Among them, a large number (46 percent) are listed as *labradores*—farmers. In addition, 60 other family heads were day laborers, those who did not own their own land, but worked the land of someone else.

Among those who were not counted as farmers, the residents of Santa Fe held a variety of different types of jobs, including adobe or brick makers, carpenters, blacksmiths, barrel makers, lumbermen, muleskinners, shoemakers, weavers, and tailors, as well as several others. Two of those included in the census listed themselves as "hunters." Santa Fe was officially home to only one schoolteacher. Also, there was only one full-time merchant included in the census. This indicates that the colonial town had remained dependent on trade goods from Mexico City. The community's workforce was still relying on trading their raw materials and natural goods—farm produce, wool, leather—for manufactured or "store" goods brought from New Spain.

presumed dead. Among those killed were 23 friars, two of every three friars in the colony.

THE RECOVERY OF SANTA FE

But Santa Fe would not be left to the Indians. The next year, large numbers of Spanish soldiers arrived in the region and reconquered the Pueblo Indians, returning most of them to Spanish control. The reestablishment of Spanish power would not happen overnight. Throughout the century that followed the 1680 Pueblo Revolt, the Spanish struggled to regain their place in the Upper Rio Grande Valley. By the 1700s, the Pueblo Indians became increasingly passive and cooperative. The Spanish

---

The economy of Santa Fe, even just 20 years before the end of the Spanish colonial period, was still based on barter and trade. There was the local trading done in and around Santa Fe. In neighboring Pecos and Taos, there were local trade fairs that drew visitors from around the Upper Rio Grande region, including Santa Fe. Money was rarely used at these trade events. Everyone knew what everything was worth when compared to something else: "For example, a bridle could be had for two buffalo hides, a horse cost twenty deerskins, and a female slave between twelve and twenty years old cost two good horses and some clothing or woven saddle blankets."*

While there were probably few stores selling finished goods in Santa Fe at the end of the eighteenth century, the town had organized a basic "factory" system of hired workers. The 1790 census reveals that 25 *obrajeros* were in business in Santa Fe. These were eighteenth-century "sweatshops" where Indians were typically put to work to produce finished products, especially blankets and other woven goods. The obrajeros were often operated by the Franciscans and the work done by the Indians, who helped to support their mission activities.

---

* David Grant Noble, *Santa Fe: History of an Ancient City* (Santa Fe, N.M.: School of American Research Press, 1989), 69.

Santa Fe is the capital of New Mexico, and according to the 2000 U.S. census, it was home to more than 65,000 residents. In the distance are the Sangre de Cristo Mountains.

had learned from many of their mistakes with the Indians and their treatment of the Pueblos was less harsh, less autocratic, and more tolerant.

Not only was Santa Fe regained as a Spanish outpost, but other Spanish settlements were established including Albuquerque, El Paso, and Santa Cruz de la Canada. Slowly, the Spanish population in New Mexico increased, passing the 5,000 mark by 1750 and growing to nearly 25,000 by the turn of the nineteenth century. During those same decades, the Pueblo population declined to about 13,000 by the mid-seventeenth century, primarily because of wars with neighboring Navajo and Apache tribes and disease. Smallpox epidemics spread throughout the

Pueblo villages from 1779 to 1780, decreasing the Indian population to around 10,000 by 1800. By that year, the Spanish had been colonizing in the region of the north for more than 250 years. They had built settlements, garrisons, presidios, villages, mission outposts, and ranches. They had carved out trails and roads that connected each to the other.

But the days of Spanish colonization were to come to an end beginning in 1810, 200 years after the founding of Santa Fe, when the Mexican people started a war for independence to overthrow the Spaniards. Nevertheless, Santa Fe continued as a viable and important community in New Mexico. Its future would extend into the present day. Today, Santa Fe stands as a multicultural monument to time and history. It is a thriving community in the American Southwest, a home to Anglos, Hispanics, and American Indians, a modern-day colony of industry and art, history and culture, where the Palace of the Governors stands at the crossroads of a region whose history is marked by those who sought God, gold, and glory, as well as those who still occupy New Mexico's ancient pueblos.

Chronology

1492 Genoan seaman Christopher Columbus accidentally "discovers" the Americas.

1513 Spanish Council of the Indies issues the Laws of Burgos, requiring Spanish officials and soldiers to treat American Indians kindly; that same year, conquistador Juan Ponce de León leads Spaniards into Florida.

Timeline

1521
Spanish complete conquest of Aztec Empire

1532
Francisco Pizarro conquers the Inca Empire in South America

1540
Francisco Coronado sent to find the cities of Cíbola

1581
Father Rodriguez reaches the pueblo of Puaray; it is here that Santa Fe will one day be established

1521

1598

1528
Pánfilo de Narváez's expedition to build a colony at the mouth of the Rio Grande fails

1536
Cabeza de Vaca rescued and returns to Mexico City

1598
Don Juan de Oñate given permission to establish a colony in New Mexico

1519 Hernán Cortéz and 600 Spanish soldiers land on the Mexican coast and begin their march to the empire of the Aztecs.

1521 The Spanish complete their conquest of the Aztec Empire.

1528 Pánfilo de Narváez's expedition to build a colony at the mouth of the Rio Grande (Rio de las Palmas) fails after a storm destroys one ship and damages the remaining three vessels; Cabeza de Vaca is among the survivors who wander the Southwest for the next eight years.

1532 Spanish leader Francisco Pizarro conquers the Inca Empire in South America.

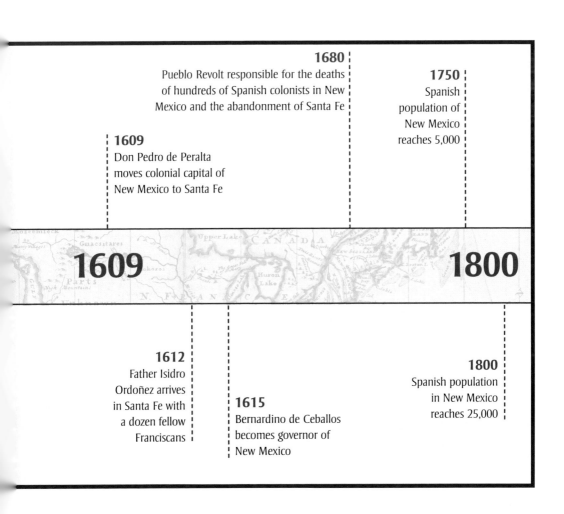

1680
Pueblo Revolt responsible for the deaths of hundreds of Spanish colonists in New Mexico and the abandonment of Santa Fe

1750
Spanish population of New Mexico reaches 5,000

1609
Don Pedro de Peralta moves colonial capital of New Mexico to Santa Fe

1609

1800

1612
Father Isidro Ordoñez arrives in Santa Fe with a dozen fellow Franciscans

1615
Bernardino de Ceballos becomes governor of New Mexico

1800
Spanish population in New Mexico reaches 25,000

1536 Cabeza de Vaca is rescued and returns to Mexico City, where he tells the viceroy of Indian stories of Cíbola.

1539 Father Marcos and Esteban head into the lands of the modern-day American Southwest in search of the Seven Cities of Cíbola; they fail to find them, but Father Marcos returns to Mexico City and claims otherwise.

1540 Viceroy Antonio de Mendoza orders conquistador Francisco Coronado to march Spanish soldiers into the Southwest in search of Cíbola.

1541 Coronado lays siege to the Pueblo settlement of Moho, which results in the deaths of hundreds of Pueblo Indians; later, Coronado marches a small party onto the Great Plains in search of Quivira.

1542 Coronado returns to Mexico City having failed to discover the Seven Cities of Cíbola; however, his men have extensively explored the Southwest, including modern-day New Mexico.

1581 Group of Franciscans, led by Father Agustin Rodriguez, travels into the Southwest to teach the Pueblo Indians; the friars reach the pueblo at Puaray and remain; it is here that Santa Fe will one day be established.

1582 Another Franciscan expedition reaches the Southwest, led by Father Bernardino Beltrán and Antonio de Espejo, a military commander; they, too, reach Puaray, but find that the friars who had arrived the previous year have been killed; Espejo will later propose to Mexico City officials that a colony be established in the Rio Grande Valley.

1590 Spanish colonists enter New Mexico to colonize without permission from the Royal Crown; word of the illegal colonizing party reaches Mexico City and is halted while their leader is punished.

1593 Another illegal expedition attempts to establish a New Mexico colony; the Leyva-Gutierrez

Expedition ends when Indians attack, killing nearly everyone.

1598 Don Juan de Oñate is given permission to establish a self-financed colony in New Mexico; the colony reaches the Valley of the Rio Grande but struggles to survive; the main settlement site is built at San Gabriel.

1607 Oñate resigns after having been investigated for mismanagement of his colony.

1609 Oñate's replacement as governor is selected, another Spanish aristocrat, Don Pedro de Peralta; he decides to move the colonial center from San Gabriel to his new capital site, Santa Fe, to be located at the confluence of the Chama River and the Rio Grande.

1610 The transfer of the Spanish capital of New Mexico to Santa Fe is completed; that same year, Father Alonso de Peinado establishes his church "headquarters" near the Santo Domingo Pueblo, south of Santa Fe.

1610–1615 The new community of Santa Fe takes root and begins to develop.

1612 Father Isidro Ordoñez arrives in Santa Fe with a dozen fellow Franciscans; he will soon challenge Governor Peralta's authority.

1613–1615 Father Ordoñez holds Peralta prisoner, claiming full authority over the New Mexico colony.

1615 A new governor is appointed to rule Santa Fe and New Mexico—Bernardino de Ceballos; he will, in time, release Peralta.

1617 Peralta is found innocent of any charges leveled against him; as for Father Ordoñez, he is ordered to Mexico City to account for his actions.

1630 A church report states that 50 friars are working in 90 Indian villages in and around Santa Fe.

1680 Massive Pueblo Revolt causes the deaths of hundreds of Spanish colonists in New Mexico and the abandonment of Santa Fe; the reestablishment of Spanish power in the region of the Upper Rio Grande will take years.

1750 Spanish population of New Mexico reaches 5,000.

1779–80 Smallpox epidemic spreads through the New Mexico pueblos, killing thousands.

1800 Spanish population in New Mexico reaches 25,000.

1810 After 200 years of colonization in New Mexico and Santa Fe, the Mexican war for independence brings an end to the Spanish colonial period in the region.

Notes

Chapter 1
1. Graham Raht, *The Romance of Davis Mountains and Big Bend Country: A History* (Odessa, Tex.: The Rahtbooks Company, 1963), 9.
2. George Daniels, ed. *The Spanish West* (New York: Time-Life Books, 1976), 26.
3. Ibid., 27.
4. Raht, 9.
5. Daniels, 7.
6. Ibid., 27.
7. Paul Horgan, *Conquistadors in North American History* (New York: Farrar, Straus and Company, 1963), 161.

Chapter 2
8. Peter Charles Hoffer, *The Brave New World: A History of Early America* (Boston: Houghton Mifflin Company, 2000), 79.
9. Horgan, *Conquistadors*, 32.
10. David Goldfield, *The American Journey, A History of the United States* (Upper Saddle River, N.J.: Prentice Hall, 2004), 21.
11. Ibid.
12. Ibid., 22.

Chapter 3
13. Tim McNeese, *The Rio Grande* (Philadelphia: Chelsea House Publishers, 2004), 29.
14. Lynn I. Perrigo, *The American Southwest: Its People and Cultures* (Albuquerque: University of New Mexico Press, 1971), 22.
15. Daniels, 29.
16. Ibid.
17. Ibid.
18. Ibid.
19. Ibid.
20. Ibid., 34.
21. W. Eugene Hollon, *The Southwest: Old and New* (Lincoln: University of Nebraska Press, 1961), 55.
22. Ibid.

Chapter 4
23. Ibid., 34.
24. Ibid., 35.
25. Ibid.
26. Ibid.
27. Horgan, *Conquistadors*, 112.
28. Ibid.
29. Ibid., 170.
30. Daniels, 35.
31. Horgan, *Conquistadors*, 170.
32. Daniels, 35.
33. Horgan, *Conquistadors*, 170–71.
34. Ibid., 171.
35. Daniels, 35.

Chapter 5
36. Ibid., 38.
37. Paul I. Wellman, *Glory, God and Gold* (Garden City, N.Y.: Doubleday & Company, Inc., 1954), 35.
38. Ibid., 36.

39. Daniels, 38.
40. Ibid., 41.
41. Ibid., 42.
42. Ibid.
43. Ibid., 43.
44. Ibid.
45. Ibid.
46. McNeese, 38.

Chapter 6

47. Perrigo, 30.
48. Ibid., 33.
49. Albert J. Nevins, *Our American Catholic Heritage* (Huntington, Ind.: Our Sunday Visitor, Inc., 1972), 61.
50. Wellman, 71.
51. Perrigo, 36.
52. John L. Kessell, *Kiva, Cross, and Crown: The Pecos Indians and New Mexico, 1540–1840* (Washington, D.C.: National Park Service, U.S. Department of the Interior, 1979), 93.
53. Perrigo, 37.

Chapter 7

54. Daniels, 44.
55. Ibid., 50.
56. McNeese, 49.
57. David Grant Noble, *Santa Fe: History of an Ancient City* (Santa Fe: School of American Research Press, 1989), 27.
58. Ibid., 28.
59. Ibid.

Chapter 8

60. Ibid., 32.
61. Kessell, 97.
62. Ibid.
63. Ibid.
64. Noble, 34.
65. Kessell, 97.
66. Noble, 36.
67. Ibid., 37.
68. Ibid.

Chapter 9

69. Perrigo, 41.
70. Daniels, 51.
71. Ibid., 52.
72. Ibid.

Bibliography

Athearn, Robert G. *The New World*. New York: Choice Publishing, 1988.

Bancroft, Hubert Howe. *History of Arizona and New Mexico, 1530–1888*. Albuquerque, N.M.: Horn & Wallace, Publishers, 1962.

Blacker, Irwin R. *Cortes and the Aztec Conquest*. New York: American Heritage Publishing Co., 1965.

Bolton, Herbert E. *Coronado: Knight of Pueblos and Plains*. Albuquerque, N.M.: The University of New Mexico Press, 1949.

Chavez, Thomas E., ed. *An Illustrated History of New Mexico*. Niwot, Colo.: University Press of Colorado, 1992.

Daniels, George, ed. *The Spanish West*. New York: Time-Life Books, 1976.

Goldfield, David. *The American Journey, A History of the United States*. Upper Saddle River, N.J.: Prentice Hall, 2004.

Hoffer, Peter Charles. *The Brave New World: A History of Early America*. Boston: Houghton Mifflin Company, 2000.

Hollon, W. Eugene. *The Southwest: Old and New*. Lincoln: University of Nebraska Press, 1961.

Horgan, Paul. *The Centuries of Santa Fe*. New York: E.P. Dutton & Company, 1956.

———. *Conquistadors in North American History*. New York: Farrar, Straus and Company, 1963.

Kessell, John L. *Kiva, Cross, and Crown: The Pecos Indians and New Mexico, 1540–1840*. Washington, D.C.: National Park Service, U.S. Department of the Interior, 1979.

McNeese, Tim. *The Rio Grande*. Philadelphia: Chelsea House Publishers, 2004.

Nevins, Albert J. *Our American Catholic Heritage*. Huntington, Ind.: Our Sunday Visitor, 1972.

Noble, David Grant. *Santa Fe: History of an Ancient City*. Santa Fe, N.M.: School of American Research Press, 1989.

Perrigo, Lynn I. *The American Southwest: Its People and Cultures.* Albuquerque: University of New Mexico Press, 1971.

Raht, Graham. *The Romance of Davis Mountains and Big Bend Country: A History.* Odessa, Tex.: The Rahtbooks Company, 1963.

Wellman, Paul I. *Glory, God and Gold.* Garden City, N.Y.: Doubleday & Company, 1954.

Further Reading

Barter, James. *The Rio Grande*. San Diego: Thomson Gale Group, 2004.

Cantor, Carrie Nichols. *Francisco Coronado*. Chanhassen, Minn.: Child's World, 2003.

Covert, Kim. *New Mexico*. Mankato, Minn.: Capstone Press, 2003.

De Angelis, Therese. *New Mexico (From Sea to Shining Sea series)*. New York: Scholastic Library Publishing, 2002.

Doak, Robin S. *Coronado*. Minneapolis, Minn.: Compass Point Books, 2001.

Early, Theresa. *New Mexico*. St. Paul, Minn.: Lerner Publishing Group, 2002.

Kummer, Patricia K. *New Mexico*. Mankato, Minn.: Capstone Press, 2002.

Lourie, Peeter. *Rio Grande: From the Rocky Mountains to the Gulf of Mexico*. Honesdale, Pa.: Boyds Mills Press, 1999.

McDaniel, Melissa. *New Mexico*. Salt Lake City, Utah: Benchmark Books, 1999.

Web sites

New Mexico Hispanic History
http://www.newmexico.org/go/loc/about/page/about-hispanicculture.html

New Mexico's Cultural Treasures
www.nmculture.org

Palace of the Governors
http://www.palaceofthegovernors.org/

Santa Fe Culture
http://www.santafe.org/Visiting_Santa_Fe/Culture/History/

Picture Credits

Index

111

About the Author

TIM MCNEESE is associate professor of history at York College in York, Nebraska, where he is in his fifteenth year of college instruction. Professor McNeese earned an associate of arts degree from York College, a bachelor of arts in history and political science from Harding University, and a master of arts in history from Missouri State University. A prolific author of books for elementary, middle and high school, and college readers, McNeese has published more than 80 books and educational materials over the past 20 years, on everything from Picasso to landmark Supreme Court decisions. His writing has earned him a citation in the library reference work *Contemporary Authors.* In 2006, McNeese appeared on the History Channel program *Risk Takers/History Makers: John Wesley Powell and the Grand Canyon.*